Stereotyping Religion

CRITIQUING RELIGION: DISCOURSE, CULTURE, POWER

Series editor: Craig Martin

Critiquing Religion: Discourse, Culture, Power publishes works that historicize both religions and modern discourses on 'religion' that treat it as a unique object of study. Using diverse methodologies and social theories, volumes in this series view religions and discourses on religion as commonplace rhetorics, authenticity narratives, or legitimating myths which function in the creation, maintenance, and contestation of social formations. Works in the series are on the cutting edge of critical scholarship, regarding 'religion' as just another cultural tool used to gerrymander social space and distribute power relations in the modern world. *Critiquing Religion: Discourse, Culture, Power* provides a unique home for reflexive, critical work in the field of religious studies.

Spirituality, Corporate Culture, and American Business:
The Neoliberal Ethic and the Spirit of Global Capital,
James Dennis LoRusso

Stereotyping Religion

Critiquing Clichés

**EDITED BY
BRAD STODDARD AND
CRAIG MARTIN**

Bloomsbury Academic
An imprint of Bloomsbury Publishing Plc

BLOOMSBURY
LONDON · OXFORD · NEW YORK · NEW DELHI · SYDNEY

Bloomsbury Academic

An imprint of Bloomsbury Publishing Plc

50 Bedford Square
London
WC1B 3DP
UK

1385 Broadway
New York
NY 10018
USA

www.bloomsbury.com

BLOOMSBURY and the Diana logo are trademarks of Bloomsbury Publishing Plc

First published 2017

© Brad Stoddard, Craig Martin and Contributors, 2017

British Library Cataloguing-in-Publication Data
A catalogue record for this book is available from the British Library.

ISBN: HB: 978-1-4742-9220-7
PB: 978-1-4742-9219-1
ePDF: 978-1-4742-9221-4
ePub: 978-1-4742-9222-1

Library of Congress Cataloging-in-Publication Data
A catalog record for this book is available from the Library of Congress.

Series design by Dani Leigh
Cover image © Yi Lu / EyeEm / gettyimages.co.uk

Series: Critiquing Religion: Discourse, Culture, Power

Typeset by Newgen Knowledge Works (P) Ltd., Chennai, India
Printed and bound in Great Britain

To find out more about our authors and books visit www.bloomsbury.com. Here you will find extracts, author interviews, details of forthcoming events and the option to sign up for our newsletters.

This book is dedicated to all of those teachers
committed to un-teaching

Contents

Contributors

Andie Alexander, who studied at the University of Alabama and CU Boulder, is pursuing her PhD in American Religious Cultures at Emory University. Her research focuses on identity construction, boundary formation, nationalism, and discourses on classification in the United States.

Leslie Dorrough Smith, PhD, is an associate professor and chair of the Department of Religious Studies and Philosophy and Director of the Women's and Gender Studies Program at Avila University. She is author of *Righteous Rhetoric: Sex, Speech, and the Politics of Concerned Women for America* (2014), and her research focuses broadly on the ways that American conservatives impact sex, gender, and reproduction policy in the United States.

Tenzan Eaghll, PhD, completed his doctoral research at the Department for the Study of Religion at the University of Toronto in 2016. He is currently a lecturer at the College of Religious Studies at Mahidol University, Thailand. His research focuses on the intersection of continental philosophy and method and theory in the study of religion, with a special focus on contemporary French thought.

Jennifer Eyl, PhD, is an assistant professor of Religion at Tufts University. She specializes in religions of the ancient Mediterranean, especially ancient Christianity. Her interests also include gender and sexuality in antiquity and theory of religion.

Rebekka King, PhD, is an assistant professor of Religious Studies at Middle Tennessee State University. Her research focuses on the negotiation of boundaries within North American Christianity. She teaches courses on method and theory, anthropology of religion, and contemporary Christianity.

James Dennis LoRusso, PhD, is a postdoctoral research associate in the Center for the Study of Religion at Princeton University. He is the author of *Spirituality, Corporate Culture, and American Business: The Neoliberal Ethic and the Spirit of Global Capital* (2017). LoRusso's work explores the intersection of religion and capitalism in twentieth- and twenty-first-century North America.

Sean McCloud, PhD, is a professor of Religious Studies (and American Studies and Communication Studies faculty affiliate) at the University of North Carolina at Charlotte. He teaches, publishes, and researches in the fields of American religions, religion and culture, and social theory. His publications include *American Possessions: Fighting Demons in the Contemporary United States* (2015); *Divine Hierarchies: Class in American Religion and Religious Studies* (2007); and *Making the American Religious Fringe: Exotics, Subversives, and Journalists, 1955–1993* (2004).

Russell T. McCutcheon, PhD, earned his doctorate at the University of Toronto in 1995 and is a professor and chair of the Department of Religious Studies, University of Alabama. His work applies social theory to the study of religion, specifically the category religion itself, examining how groups use classifications systems to create and contest social rank and privilege.

Steven W. Ramey, PhD, is a professor in Religious Studies at the University of Alabama, where he also directs the Asian Studies Program. In his first book, *Hindu, Sufi, or Sikh* (2008), he analyzes the practices and contested definitions of communities identified as Sindhi Hindus. He has extended this analysis of identification to reflect on issues in academic and public discourse surrounding the category religion and issues of identifications in various contexts.

Matt Sheedy, PhD, lectures in the Department of Religion at the University of Manitoba, Winnipeg, and is associate editor of the *Bulletin for the Study of Religion*. His research interests include critical social theory, theories of secularism, atheism and science versus religion in the public realm, as well as representations of Christianity, Islam, and Native traditions in popular and political culture. He is currently working on a book that offers a critique of Jürgen Habermas's theory of religion in the public sphere.

Robyn Faith Walsh, PhD, is an assistant professor of New Testament and Early Christianity at the University of Miami (Florida). Her research interests include the letters of Paul, the history of the interpretation of the synoptic problem, Greco-Roman archaeology, and cognitive science. She is currently working on the influence of Romanticism on the field of early Christian studies and authorship practices in antiquity.

Acknowledgments

We would first like to thank all of the contributors to this volume; they were incredibly tolerant of our requests for revisions. Thanks also go to Lalle Pursglove at Bloomsbury, both for her support of this project and for her patience with our multiple requests to extend the manuscript's deadline.

Brad would like to thank his colleagues at McDaniel College, Florida State University, and those throughout the academic study of religion, particularly those who exposed him to many of the ideas that appear in this book. He would also like to thank all of the contributors. It has been a pleasure and an honor to edit a book that includes many of the people who have informed his thinking on the academic study of religion. Finally, he would like to acknowledge and thank Stacy, Mailey, and Addison for much more than he can list here.

Craig would like to thank all of the students at St. Thomas Aquinas College that he's had the opportunity to work with over the last eight years; we would not be able to identify the pedagogical needs this volume hopes to address without the students who struggle with what we teach because we fail to make our background knowledge explicit for them. Craig would also like to acknowledge his many colleagues in religious studies, far too many to count (but you know who you are!); the passionate conversations and exchanges we've had in publications, on Facebook, or over a beer at the annual conference have always been central to maintaining the spark of intellectual curiosity that drives our work. Last, Craig would like to thank Donovan Schaefer and Jeremy Vecchi for working on a previous iteration of this idea for a book over a decade ago; although that volume never came to fruition, our many discussions about the project helped make this one possible.

Introduction

Brad Stoddard and Craig Martin

It is clichéd to begin a book about a concept by pointing to its dictionary definition; however, in this case the dictionary definition is instructive. According to *Merriam-Webster*, a cliché is "a phrase or expression that has been used so often that it is no longer original or interesting." Another dictionary defines a cliché as "a phrase or opinion that is overused and betrays a lack of original thought." Still other dictionaries offer similar definitions: a cliché is a common expression or idea that is often repeated but not interrogated or questioned. Of course, if clichés were nothing more than oft-repeated, superficial phrases, they probably wouldn't be worth addressing at length, and this book wouldn't need to exist. However, clichés sometimes have very powerful political effects and thus deserve serious consideration.

Consider that during the early half of the twentieth century, Nazi propaganda claimed that Jews were alien infiltrators of Germany, racially inferior to Aryans, and a threat to German Aryan purity. A number of stereotypes or clichés circulated widely about Jews, including the view that they were greedy, wealthy, and manipulative. During that time, Adolf Hitler endorsed and cited a forged document called *The Protocols of the Elders of Zion*. Originally from Russia, but widely translated and circulated throughout Europe, *The Protocols* was said to have been written by Jews and described a secret Jewish plot to take over the world; for Hitler, *The Protocols* offered proof that the Jews were a true threat to German national unity. In retrospect, it is clear that the accumulation of these stereotypes about Jews and the Jewish religion over time was an essential part of persuading Germans to accept Nazi leadership over the nation. Stereotypes and clichés are powerful political tools. While none of the clichés about religion in this volume have effects as powerful as those that fueled the Holocaust, they all have real social and political effects.

Many of our contemporary views about religion have their origin in early modern political propaganda. For instance, briefly consider the cliché that "religion is a private matter." Clearly, many of those institutions we refer to as "religions" do have a wide variety of public effects. Just to offer one example, American evangelical Christians have for decades been actively involved in American politics, as they attempt to have legislatures pass laws that reflect their religious, social, or political views. Similar examples of overtly political religion are found in Buddhism, Hinduism, Islam, and all of the so-called world religions. Frankly, the cliché is completely false. However, if we study the history of early modern European politics—from 1517, when the Protestant Reformation began, to around 1700—we see that there were many struggles between kings, the Catholic Church, and the newly formed Protestant churches. For some time, kings who were allied with the Catholic Church would send police to confiscate Protestant Bibles, books, and other literature, to disrupt the distribution of Protestant propaganda. In response, Martin Luther—the most important figure of the Protestant Reformation— argued in some of his writings that religion was essentially a private matter, which did not in any way affect the state, and as such those Catholic kings should leave Protestant churches to do their work in peace. "Religion is a private matter" was said over and over again to persuade kings to change their policies toward religious minorities. Those Protestant churches, like contemporary evangelical Protestants, were themselves greatly involved in influencing politics, so—again—the cliché was false. However, the fact that it was false didn't prevent it from being a powerful political tool. Indeed, over time, Protestants succeeded in earning the right not to have their work directly interfered with by kings. Clichés may be false, but they're often useful.

Independently of their particular social or political effects, all of the clichés discussed here tend to discourage critical thinking about the subject matters at hand. Psychologists have long since demonstrated that humans tend to pay attention to evidence that conforms to the stereotypes they hold and to ignore evidence that contradicts their preferred stereotypes; this is called "confirmation bias." For instance, if you hold the stereotype that "women are bad drivers," you'll easily find evidence that supports your stereotype. No doubt some women are bad drivers, but what about the many women who are good drivers? Confirmation bias encourages you to ignore them. This type of bias tends to prevent us from considering and evaluating the evidence available to us. Along the same lines, if we take for granted the cliché that "religion is intrinsically violent," we're likely to ignore the many groups we would typically refer to as religious—such as the Quakers—who actively support pacifism. As scholars of religion, how sophisticated can our work be if we're ignoring the evidence that goes contrary to our stereotypes? Scholars of religion who go about their studies without interrogating their stereotypes tend to find little more than what they want to find.

Before we can produce critical, sophisticated scholarly work, we must become conscious of the stereotypes we hold and set them aside. Interrogating our clichés is crucial preparatory work; it is for this reason that we, as college professors, have to do more than a little *un-teaching* before teaching. Clearing away the clichés that clutter our minds is quite possibly the first and most important step to doing sophisticated academic work.

* * *

Stereotyping Religion: Critiquing Clichés attempts to move the conversation beyond the common clichés by making the clichés themselves the object of academic study. In each of the following ten chapters, the authors isolate and analyze one of the more common clichés about religion. Every chapter includes a discussion of the origins of the cliché, the social and political work it served in the past and continues to serve in the present, and where the stereotype appears in both scholarly works and popular culture. Though each scholar addresses a unique cliché, several common themes emerge.

First, as the scholars in this book suggest, although the clichés may present themselves as timeless truths, each cliché has a specific history. Each cliché emerged at a specific moment in history and found a group of people who accepted it as fact. The scholars in this book highlight these histories, grounding them in the sociocultural, historical, and political circumstances that informed the early uses of the clichés and that motivated particular people to embrace them. It is not a coincidence that specific clichés emerged at particular moments in history; rather, historical developments create new social, cultural, political, and even economic circumstances that render each cliché both possible and desirable for specific people responding to those particular circumstances. To advance our thinking about individual clichés, the essays in this book highlight these histories and sociopolitical circumstances that provided ripe conditions for the individual clichés.

In addition to summarizing the history of each cliché, this book draws attention to the people or groups who created and who favor the individual clichés. By refocusing our attention to the people who develop and support the cliché (as opposed to merely examining the validity of the cliché itself), readers will learn that individual clichés typically serve the interests of the people who created and circulated them, as the clichés describe religion in a manner consistent with the curator's interests. For example, if you encounter a person who already believes that religions are basically crutches people use to provide meaning to otherwise empty and pointless lives, would you expect this person to embrace the cliché that all religions make people moral, or would he believe that all religions are bullshit? Conversely, if you encounter a person who already believes that religious ethics provide the foundation of citizenship, which cliché would she most likely embrace? Would she think that all religions are bullshit or that religions make people moral? The answer in both examples is obviously the latter, as the individuals in both hypothetical situations embrace the cliché that fits their assumptions about religion, or in a way that is self-serving. The essays in this book provide accessible and clear examples that highlight how people deploy specific clichés, not because they are *right* but because they allow the people who use the cliché to frame all "religion" as they perceive it.

The authors in this book also highlight a third common theme as they explore the potential problems and assumptions that are associated with each cliché. Each cliché is persuasive only if we ignore the evidence that undermines it or that reveals its limitations.

Each of the following eleven authors provide detailed analyses of the major problems and counterevidences that belie each cliché.

This book serves the additional goal of introducing readers to some of the more common clichés they might not have encountered. Certain clichés are more popular among particular groups of people. For example, theists (i.e., people who believe that a god exists) are more likely to encounter the "religion concerns the transcendent" cliché. This idea might be so powerful and ubiquitous in their social circles that they might not encounter other common ideas about religion, such as the idea that "religion is inherently violent." Conversely, some atheists who wholeheartedly embrace the idea that "religion is inherently violent" might not encounter the common idea that "knowledge about religion leads to tolerance." While these individuals (and their larger social groups) might lack knowledge of the other clichés, millions of people embrace them. This book, then, provides an introduction to and overview of ten of the more common clichés that some readers might not encounter but that others wholeheartedly endorse. Most of these clichés undoubtedly have a Western and, more specifically, an American bias, so this book specifically addresses the more common clichés prevalent in American discourses.

* * *

Several of the following chapters situate the clichés discussed in relation to early modern European political thought, theories of secularization, and the popularization of atheism. Some background knowledge on these common issues and old debates will help readers contextualize the discussions in the following chapters.

Many of our clichés about religion come from the development of the ideology of political liberalism in early modern Europe and, as such, carry with them connotations or assumptions that are centuries old. It is important to note that by "liberal," we do not mean the opposite of "conservative," as the term is typically used in contemporary political debates. Rather, liberalism is the political theory that followed and displaced the ideology of absolute monarchy. Liberal theorists argued that the citizens of a state had a right to rule themselves democratically and, additionally, that the citizens should have a number of civil liberties, such as freedom of speech, freedom to assemble, the right to personal property, and so forth. As should be clear, both contemporary liberals and contemporary conservatives accept "liberalism" in this sense.

This ideology of political liberalism was formed following the wars between kings, Catholics, and Protestants mentioned earlier, and thus it is no surprise that one of the most important civil liberties bundled into liberal political theory was the freedom of religion. The theory of religion assumed by liberal theorists went something like this: Religious institutions—specifically, Christian churches—were concerned with preparing people's souls for the afterlife (i.e., saving them from hell), while state institutions were concerned with people's bodies and their property. Thus the authority of the state was limited to, first, ensuring that crimes against persons or property were prohibited and, second, protecting citizens' civil liberties against the government. Christian ministers, by contrast, had authority only over teaching the gospel. Insofar as the eternal fate of one's soul in principle had nothing to do with one's body, one's personal property, or the administration of the state, rulers could consider religion a private matter for individuals to work out with their ministers. In "A Letter Concerning Toleration," John Locke famously wrote,

> The church itself is a thing absolutely separate and distinct from the commonwealth. The boundaries on both sides are fixed and immovable. He jumbles heaven and earth together, the things most remote and opposite, who mixes these societies, which are, in their original, end, business, and everything, perfectly distinct, and infinitely different from each other. (Locke 2003, 226)

Of course, "separation of church and state" wouldn't have made much sense to late medieval European kings, since they all had complicated ties to the Catholic church's empire, but over the course of a couple of centuries, liberal political theorists were successful in making "separation of church and state" a common sense ideal. Several of the clichés discussed in later chapters—especially the idea that religion is a private matter, concerns the transcendent, or is merely a "belief system" unrelated to the social world—implicitly depend on this political theory of the nature and proper goal of religion.

In addition, anti-Catholic Protestant propaganda influenced several of the clichés. According to the Protestant Reformers, Catholics were insincere followers of the church; they would go through empty or meaningless Catholic rituals, sin to their heart's content, and then buy indulgences from the church to pay off their sin. In addition, from the Protestant perspective, lay Catholics were largely ignorant of the contents of the Bible. In contrast to their view of Catholics, Protestants emphasized the importance of reading the Bible (the Protestants were responsible for making the Bible widely available in languages other than Latin), honestly confessing the doctrines found therein and developing a sincere devotion to God that went beyond mere ritual observance. As the Protestant view of "true Christianity" was popularized, Protestantism became the default model for what "religion" was supposed to be like. Simultaneously, as European colonialism spread and Europeans began to discover other forms of culture across the world that they considered "religions," they judged them on the basis of whether those "religions" were like Protestantism: Did they have a sacred text, did they develop doctrines on the basis of that text, and did they hold sincere beliefs over and above ritual observance? The Europeans that ended up in India rather liked the many ancient and sacred texts held dear by elite Hindus. By contrast, the Europeans that ended up in West Africa thought the people there were "primitive savages": they performed empty magic rituals, had no Bible, and recited no doctrine. For all practical purposes, the Protestant ideal became the measuring stick against which other cultures were judged.

Going back to the liberal political theorists for a moment, it's important to note that, as they claimed "religion" was "private," they began to consider "public" matters by contrast in some way as essentially "nonreligious" or "secular." For peace and stability, ideally states must be "secular" rather than aligned with particular "religious" institutions. "Secular" eventually became an adjective that simply meant "nonreligious." Later, in the twentieth century, scholars developed a theory of "secularization," which, although it uses the term "secular," meant something a bit different. By the end of the twentieth century, many European Christians had stopped going to church, and many of them even stopped identifying as "Christian." Rather, an increasing number of people—especially in the United Kingdom—began to identify as agnostic or atheist. Scholars of religion wanted to be able to explain this decline in church attendance, and they called it "secularization." For these scholars, through the process of secularization, people were increasingly becoming "nonreligious." In this more contemporary sense, "secular" comes to mean not just that the state is nonreligious, but that the citizenry is as well. These scholars offered a variety of theories to explain why that was the case. Some claimed that "science" or "reason" was increasingly replacing religion, which—on this view—was regarded more or less as outdated superstition. Others claimed that as we became a more global society, interacting with people from other nations and being exposed to other beliefs, people began to question the taken-for-granted authority of their own religion. That is, as European Christians increasingly became familiar with Muslims, Buddhists, and Hindus, they started to doubt that Christianity was necessarily the "right" religion. In any case, whichever theory was used to explain why people were becoming less religious or more secular, it was widely assumed that secularization was irreversible and would eventually result in religion disappearing from society altogether. Some of the clichés discussed in this volume—especially the idea that religion is bullshit—have background assumptions tied to this theory of secularization.

At the same time that people gradually began to consider themselves secular or nonreligious, atheism became more normalized. Increasingly, people could identify as agnostic or atheist without suffering social stigma (by contrast, in the seventeenth century one could be arrested for publicly espousing atheism). The rise of atheism carried with it many negative caricatures of religions. Religion began to be viewed as irrational, childish, or culturally backward. According to some popular atheist stereotypes, religious authorities are essentially power hungry and controlling, and their followers are suckers or dupes. "Organized religion" became a pejorative phrase; organized religion was essentially a bad thing for some reason or another. Similarly, "faith" lost many of its positive connotations and began to carry negative ones.

In the first decade of the twenty-first century, a number of critics began producing a body of literature that helped establish a view that was eventually called "New Atheism"; the most important of these critics were Sam Harris, Christopher Hitchens, and the famous biologist Richard Dawkins. They produced titles such as *The End of Faith, God Is Not Great: How Religion Poisons Everything*, and *The God Delusion*. For these New Atheists, religion is not only false but also quite possibly evil. As Dawkins wrote in *The God Delusion*, "Faith can be very very dangerous, and deliberately to implant it into the vulnerable mind of an innocent child is a grievous wrong" (Dawkins 2008, 348). Contrary to the view that religion makes people moral, the atheist caricature suggests that religion makes people immoral. These sorts of assumptions underlie several of the clichés discussed in this volume.

Historical context is crucial for making sense of stereotypes about religion, and thus keeping in mind the liberal political theory of religion, the idealization of Protestantism, and the theory of secularization should make the arguments in the following chapters easier to understand.

* * *

Stereotyping Religion offers a summary, analysis, and critique of ten of the more common clichés about religion in America and Western Europe. In the chapters that follow, James Dennis LoRusso and Robyn Faith Walsh demonstrate how "everyone has a faith" and "religion is a private matter" can indirectly reinforce Protestant values, and Tenzan Eaghll shows how "learning about religion leads to tolerance" carries with it a type of Christian ethnocentrism. Steven W. Ramey shows how "religions are mutually exclusive" can be used to control populations with a certain sort of identity politics, and Jennifer Eyl shows how "religion makes people moral" may be used to ensure social conformity in a variety of ways. Matt Sheedy describes how "religions are intrinsically violent" can be used to legitimate violence against populations that are identified as religious. In their chapters, Leslie Dorrough Smith, Andie Alexander, and Russell T. McCutcheon argue that the clichés "religion concerns the transcendent" and "I'm spiritual but not religious" are power moves that legitimate the authority of the speaker who uses them. Similarly, Rebekkah King demonstrates how "religion is bullshit" tells us more about the person who uses the cliché than about religion itself. Finally, Sean McCloud shows how "religions are belief systems" falsely portrays cultural traditions as monolithic wholes.

Collectively, these essays combine to tell a larger story about the various ways that people imagine or think about religion. They do not, however, offer an answer to the questions that will undoubtedly arise: What, then, *is* religion? How can we describe its central characteristics? If these clichés are somehow problematic, as the authors repeatedly suggest, then what's a *better* way of thinking about religion? The astute reader might have noticed—and we would like to suggest—that perhaps all such generalizations are suspect. After all, *any* generalizing statement about religion faces the same sort of issues that the contributors identified in this volume. Perhaps generalizations like "all religions are X" are just as problematic as generalizations like "all women are X," or "all black people are X." It is our hope that readers, when confronted with a generalizing claim about religion, will apply the tools that they've learned in this volume. When faced with a stereotype, consider its historical and political context: With this claim, who is trying to persuade whom of what? Who stands to gain and who stands to lose if the claim is received as true? Ultimately, it appears that stereotypes and clichés about religion likely tell us more about the people who repeat the clichés than they do about religion.

1

"Religions are belief systems"

Sean McCloud

The problem, then, is not whether belief exists—this is difficult to determine—but whether religion must be represented as something that derives from belief, as something with external manifestation that can ultimately be traced back to an inner assent to a cognitive proposition, as a state of mind that produces practice. Donald Lopez Jr. (1998, 34)

My undergraduate religion courses are full of belief. By this I mean that, for most students, *belief* is the primary default concept when it comes to religion. At the beginning of the semester, I often have a class work in small groups to think about and report on what they think we will be studying in the course. For example, if the class is Religion and American Culture, I have the students discuss in small groups what their starting conceptions/definitions of *religion*, *American*, and *culture* might be. When reporting back to the larger class on their group's conceptions of religion, students overwhelmingly say things such as, "religion is a set of beliefs," "religion is about what you really believe," and "religion is a system of beliefs." Even when students add a term such as *ritual*, *belief* is almost always the first term in the working definition.

But it isn't just college students. Many of us have been socially habituated to assume that the thing we call religion is first and

foremost about belief and—even more—that what one believes is
the basis for an individual's action, whether that action is seen as
religious or not. Additionally, religion and belief are often connected
in ways that can serve political purposes. For example, we hear
politicians touting their deeply believed values as being primary
to their qualification as candidates for government office. We see
journalists and pundits asserting that terrorist acts occur because
of the perpetrators' religious beliefs. Sometimes, conversely, we
hear politicians, religious leaders, and pundits argue that terrorist
actions could never be religious because that would go against
the "true" beliefs of the religion. And when scandals occur—for
example, in 2006, when conservative evangelical leader and gay
civil rights opponent Ted Haggard was discovered to have had a
three-year sexual relationship with a male escort—people see the
dissonance between stated belief and action as an opportunity to
lob accusations of hypocrisy at the person in question (Banerjee
2007). The point here is not to contest whether Haggard could be
correctly dubbed a hypocrite but that we are often quick to assume
that beliefs spur actions, rather than it being the opposite, or
some interaction of factors. Belief is a term (like all terms) that is
constructed, contextual, and chameleon-like. And its connection to
religion, a term just as constructed and contextual, seems natural
and fixed. The purpose of this chapter is not to suggest that belief
has nothing to do with the social formations that scholars and
participants refer to as religions, nor is its purpose to deny that some
institutional forms of religion have dogmas that might be described
as "belief systems." Instead, it suggests that we need to reflect on
and interrogate the reasons why the notion that religion is about
belief and that religions are belief systems are such comfortable
and often unquestioned assumptions.

   In brief, I argue that the trope that religion is a belief system
suggests a particular bounded and cohesive institutional social
formation that involves agents who think and act in rational and
predictable ways based on their religion's doctrines or dogmas. By
this I mean that such a conception narrows the notion of religion to
religious institutions and doctrines, while simultaneously assuming
that humans are coherent and consistent beings whose actions can
be understood primarily in light of the rules and codes they choose
to adhere by. Such a conception does two kinds of work. First, it

posits a coherent and consistent self, one that can be tracked over time and morally judged by the consistency of his values. Second, the assumption that religions are belief systems tends to preference a definition of religion as a set of doctrines set forth by institutions that one follows. In what follows, I discuss the problems and foreclosures involved in focusing on belief and conceiving religions as belief systems.

The problems with belief

The idea that religion is primarily about belief emerged in the wake of the Protestant Reformation, the fracturing of the Catholic Church, and the religious wars that accompanied these developments. As Talal Asad noted, it was in this environment in the seventeenth century that Lord Herbert offered a theory of Natural Religion centered on belief, ethics, and practices (Asad 1993, 40). This conception of religion proved appealing to Protestants, who appealed to sincerely held religious belief to distinguish themselves from what they perceived as the empty (and pagan-influenced) ritual that dominated Catholicism—rituals that, Protestants alleged, were performed without sincerity. Such a definition, and the many that followed that similarly located religious belief as the primary object of religion itself, ignores that, for many so-called religions, belief is often subordinated to ritual or action (certain forms of Judaism, Catholicism, and Zen Buddhism offer cases in point). The American religious historian Robert Orsi once recounted his students' negative reactions when they were exposed to a version of religion that was not centered on belief.

Orsi described how he showed his students images and discussed with them a popular Catholic religious site known as the Lourdes of the Bronx. The grotto at St. Lucy's was built in 1939 and continues to draw pilgrims who come to pray and take the holy water from the spring supplied by a New York City tap. "The water in the Bronx is treated by those who come for it as Lourdes water," Orsi writes, "and it is also believed to be miraculous" (Orsi 1997, 3). Most of his class, upon hearing how people use the city tap water with the hope of healing bodies and fixing cars, expressed distaste. Many even went so far as to suggest that such supernatural actions couldn't possibly be "real" religion. For his students, as for many contemporary Americans, religion is "private and interior, not shamelessly public; mystical, not ritualistic; intellectually consistent and reasonable, not ambivalent and contradictory" (6). In other words, "true religion" is about private beliefs that are rational and consistent.

Yet, to the extent that the academic study of religion is the study of humans, in groups and as individuals, and what they think and do that they, or we as scholars, call religion, our personal opinions, likes, and dislikes are probably not the best tools to draw the boundaries of our examinations. And though the image of humans as autonomous, conscious, rational, and consistent may be comforting to many, studies suggest that individual actions and convictions are not consistent over time, but instead are contextual to specific places, times, and social groups. In *Talk of Love: How Culture Matters*, the sociologist Ann Swidler found that "most people do not actually have a single, unified set of attitudes or beliefs and that searching for such unified beliefs was the wrong way to approach the study of culture" (Swidler 2001, 4). In her discussions with research participants, for example, Swidler noted that they used two contrasting vocabularies for talking about love, depending on what question they were asked. When asked to discuss what love was, individuals frequently talked about it as a free and voluntary choice that people enter into, asserting that love knows no bounds and creates no boundaries. But if posed with a question about why one should stay married, or whether one should have to care for a deathly ill loved one, the same individuals shifted to a language of necessary commitments and obligations (25–31). Another example, outside of Swidler's study, would be someone who says his pro-life stance requires him to be against abortion, yet at the same time argues in support of the death penalty in the name of just punishment. Swidler's participants talking about love and the pro-life/pro-death penalty example suggests that, rather than holding singular and consistent beliefs over time, "people run through different parts of their cultural repertoires, selecting those parts that correspond to the situation or exemplary problem ... that currently holds their attention" (25).

"Belief" is thus a problematic concept because it can presuppose that humans hold to concepts and ideas that are all coherent and logically consistent over time. But it is also troublesome because it focuses on conscious thought so much that it disregards the equally (if not more) significant manner that "religions" engage our bodies and emotions in ways that we are not always conscious of. Rather than "belief," one could just as easily relate how religion involves "embodied dispositions." Embodied dispositions are forces of habit, or as the anthropologist Jessica Johnson calls them, "convictions unbound by doctrine," that foment actions and emotions (Johnson 2015, 2018). In other words, individuals are the products of their past histories. Our pasts have filled us with habits and dispositions that make us feel, act, and react in certain ways. Because of this, religious things—whether it be a song, an image, speaking in tongues—may make us feel comfort, discomfort, pleasure, fear, anxiety. Embodied dispositions, those historical habits that foment comfort, discomfort, and convictions, work to attract or repel individuals toward or away from certain ideas and practices that might be defined as "religious" in ways that are much more complicated and affective than the trope of belief allows.

The problem with "religions are belief systems": The case of American religions

The religious studies scholar Donald Lopez Jr. has noted that, historically, "scholars of religion and anthropologists have almost invariably defined religion in terms of belief or perhaps beliefs and practices, those deeds motivated by belief" (Lopez Jr. 1998, 21). While academic definitions of religion are varied, rarely is the term belief omitted from them. What's more, it is common to see religion defined as not just about belief and doctrine, but rather as a coherent system of beliefs and doctrines (as well as other elements). Perhaps one of the most classic examples is from the early twentieth-century scholar Emile Durkheim, whose famous definition reads, "a religion is a unified system of beliefs and practices relative to sacred things, that is to say, things set apart and forbidden—beliefs and practices which unite into one single moral community called a Church, all those who adhere to them" (Durkheim 1915, 62).

In assuming that religion is best described as a system of beliefs, the concept of religion can easily become tied to a set doctrine, scripted practices, and an institution that controls such things. But connecting "religion" to these items ignores other ways that it can just as easily be conceived. This is not surprising. After all, devising categories and then analyzing them is part of what scholars do. But if we acknowledge that conceptions of "religion" are always constructs that focus on certain things to the exclusion of others, then it becomes apparent that focusing on religion as a "system of beliefs" that are tied to an ecclesiastical (i.e., "churchly") institution prevents us from recognizing that modern American religious practices could just as easily be described in other ways. For example, one could examine polling data (and stick with defining religion narrowly as somehow involving "supernatural" powers, beings, and things, keeping in mind that many definitions of religion, are much broader than this) to argue that what scholars describe as American religions are not just systems of belief, but rather amalgams of practices and ideas pieced together by individuals in certain contexts.

Most Americans pick, mix, and combine a variety of religious and cultural idioms to find what works for them in their everyday lives. This includes not only most of those identified as "nones" (i.e., those not affiliated with religious institutions) in recent polls but also those who do identify with a particular religious institution. For those interested in neat categorizations and institutional definitions of religion as belief systems, this makes things a bit messy. I don't point this out to suggest that focusing on the combinative practices of American religions necessarily provides a more accurate description than studies that narrow religion to a conventional set of churches and traditions. Both, of course, are scholarly constructs that allow us to concentrate on certain issues and trends. But I do suggest that, in terms of a broad public discourse about religion, to focus on it solely as an institution with a coherent and consistent system of beliefs has the unintended consequence of promoting views that narrow the boundaries of American religion to a predictable set of dominant, mostly Christian, groups—leaving the rest ignored. But surveys and fieldwork studies suggest that any simple conclusions made about something out there that we call religion relate as much to how we define that term as to what Americans might actually be doing.

The American religious historian Robert Orsi argues that "the study of religions in the United States is necessarily the study of improvisations" (Orsi 1993, 1). One prominent form such improvisation has taken is the dynamic picking, mixing, and fusing of religious and cultural materials. While religious traditions and institutions remain a large and important scholarly focus, in the last few decades social scientists, historians, specialists in Asian immigrant religions, ethnographers, and folklorists have also attended to the ways that individuals—and some of the religious movements to which they belong—have improvised new religious blends from cultural materials available to them.

Studies suggest that some things have changed in American religion since World War II. The major ones include the numerical decline of so-called mainline Protestant denominations and the growth in theologically conservative ones (as well as more theologically open ones, such as neo-paganism), the increase in "switching" religious groups during one's lifespan, and a rising cohort of Americans who belong to no religious groups and get disparately lumped together under the moniker "nones" (Roof and McKinney 1987, Wuthnow 1988, Roof 1999, Kosmin et. al. 2009, Chaves 2011, Pew Research Center 2012). Add to these a host of other changes, including the increased presence of Asian religions (enabled by a 1965 change in immigration laws), the expanded access to religious materials enabled by mass media technologies, the rise of evangelical seekers and megachurches along the beltways of New South and Midwestern cities, the declining importance of denominational identity and theological particularities, the deepening connections between white evangelicals and the Republican Party, and the increase in those who tell pollsters that they believe in angels, demons, and ghosts (McCloud 2007, Jagel 2013).

In assessing changes since the 1950s and 1960s, many studies have focused on the move from institutional to individual authority in American religion. Well reflected in Robert Fuller's book title, *Spiritual, But Not Religious: Understanding Unchurched America*, polled Americans have been increasingly suspicious of religious institutions and simultaneously self-reliant and subjective in their spirituality (Fuller 2001). In 1985, Robert Bellah and his colleagues published *Habits of the Heart: Individualism and Commitment in American Life*. They argued that the language of individualism dominated

American life generally and provided the religious example of Sheila Larson, an interviewee who called her combinative and idiosyncratic religious faith "Sheilaism" (Bellah et al. 1985). Individualism and subjective authority is also the subject of Phillip Hammond's *Religion and Personal Autonomy: The Third Disestablishment in America*. Hammond asserts that religious institutions have been changed and even weakened in terms of moral influence due to the growth in Americans' commitments to personal authority and experience (Hammond 1992). In *Spiritual Marketplace: Baby Boomers and the Remaking of American Religion*, Wade Clark Roof suggests the emergence of an individualized, contemporary "quest culture." The current period, Roof suggests, is filled with religious seekers who actively shop in a spiritual marketplace of religious goods for beliefs and practices that best suit their shifting interests and concerns (Roof 1999). More recently, the sociologist Meredith McGuire has shown how the everyday, lived religious practices of individuals entail various forms of religious blending (McGuire 2008, 188–99).

While the empirical evidence predominantly shows that people blend forms of culture rather than accept a monolithic orthodoxy, these studies arguably leave out how blending is determined by larger sociocultural, political, and economic trends. For example, in *Capitalizing Religion*, Craig Martin notes that the rhetoric of individualism seen in such studies "masks the extent to which 'individuals' are collectively constituted" by the material forces of consumer capitalism in which they live their lives rather than accurately representing a shift to individual autonomy with regard to religious practice (Martin 2014, 6). Specifically, Martin argues that "many of those forms that scholars identify as 'individual religion' or 'spirituality' constitute individuals specifically as subjects of capitalism by encouraging consumerism, productivity, and quietism with respect to the economic and political structures" (6). I note this to suggest that, while the studies I cite do a good job of showing the combinative practices of many Americans, they often fail to see how such activity has been socially habituated—become embodied dispositions—through the material and social conditions of living within contemporary capitalism.

Picking, mixing, and combining a variety of religious and cultural ideas about the supernatural is a noticeable part of the trends that the aforementioned scholars discuss, and such activities are revealed in polling from institutes such as Pew, Harris, and others. A December 2009 Pew Poll was titled "Many Americans Mix Multiple Faiths" (Pew Research Center 2009). While this poll was touted as striking, its findings replicated previous studies that had been conducted as far back as the early 1980s. The Pew Center wrote that "many ... blend Christianity with eastern or New Age beliefs such as reincarnation, astrology, and the presence of spiritual energy in physical objects.... And sizable minorities of all major religious groups," the writers added, "say they have experienced supernatural phenomena, such as being in touch with the dead or ghosts." In terms of specific numbers, 29 percent reported that they had recently been in touch with the dead, 26 percent said there was spiritual energy in objects such as trees, 25 percent found astrological information helpful, and 24 percent said they believed in reincarnation, specifically that when they died, they would be reborn in a physical form on earth to live again. In all, the December 2009 Pew Poll found that 65 percent of all those interviewed "express belief in or report having experience with at least one of these diverse supernatural phenomena" (Pew Research Center 2009).

An interesting case in point, reflected in this and other studies, is reincarnation. Since the late 1970s, anywhere from 19 to 40 percent of Americans polled said they believed in it. On the low end, this includes an early 1990s study in which 19 percent who were identified as *loyalists* to their religious traditions still believed in reincarnation (Roof 1993, 202). On the high end, one 2003 Harris Poll found that 40 percent of all twenty-five- to twenty-nine-year-olds believed in it (Taylor 2003). Even the lowest number, 19 percent, is a much higher percentage than the small number of Americans—probably 1 percent to at most 2 percent—who belong to religious traditions such as Buddhism and Hinduism that formally hold reincarnation doctrines.

Both scholarly studies and research polling suggest that combinative religious beliefs and practices appear throughout all of the sites in which individuals enact what gets popularly dubbed faith. While the eclectic and innovative neo-pagan and New Age practices provide two obvious cases, other examples have appeared within religious denominations, ranging from a Conservative Rabbi who utilizes Zen Buddhist techniques in his synagogue to the Reverend Matthew Fox's Techno Cosmic Mass, which explicitly synthesizes world religious traditions (Cimino and Lattin 1998, 22, 25). Fieldwork studies have also revealed blends. The folklorist Jody Shapiro Davie, for example, showed how members of one Presbyterian women's Bible study group mixed their vibrant beliefs in and experiences of the supernatural with Jungian psychology, while Lynn Schofield Clark demonstrated how mass media portrayals of the supernatural interacted with and played a role in the religious beliefs and practices of teenagers and young adults (Davie 1995, Clark 2003). In all of these cases, the practitioners pick, mix, and combine in ways that result in unique collages. While these things may not look doctrinally orthodox to those interested in such things, they are part of the lived religious practices of those seeking the efficacious, by which I mean here those things that can help them explain, administer healing, and provide guidance in everyday life. Religion, in this case, is not a coherent and fixed system of beliefs or doctrines, but rather a shifting amalgam of practices and ideas— a repertoire of items from which one takes as different personal and social situations arise.

Conclusion

"I don't know. I am Buddhist. But I am Christian. I guess
    I am both."
"Sometimes I am Buddhist, sometimes I am Christian."
"I am both."

These quotations come from the documentary *Blue Collar and Buddha* (1986). The film focuses on the Laotian refugee community of Rockford, Illinois, in the early 1980s. Specifically, it examines the difficulties of the immigrant community in adjusting to their new environs or, perhaps more accurately, the difficulties of some Rockford citizens in adjusting to the Laotians. The documentary records the acute violence directed at the community's Buddhist Temple, which, in the span of months, was attacked by someone using a high-powered rifle and, later, a pipe bomb. In it, racism and religious prejudice combine in shameful ways as some Rockfordians showed little reluctance to spew their hatred on camera for posterity.

But the quotations I use come from a set of interviews with Laotians at the Buddhist Temple, who are asked what religion they are. The question was spurred by the fact that the same people who could be seen at the Buddhist Temple were also present in the Christian Church pews on Sunday mornings. One is struck by the straight-forwardness of the answers. One may also be struck by how such answers point to something more complex than the conception of religion as a belief system.

So, rather than by adhering to set and non-negotiable systems of belief, Americans live by picking, mixing, and combining a variety of religious and cultural idioms (within a sphere of materials constrained by their social locations) to find what works for them in everyday life. But, one can ask, so what? Well, in terms of the academic study of religion and the teaching of American religions, one simple answer would be that attention to the blending of religious, supernatural, and other cultural elements—examining how humans act in and on their worlds by combining—should give us pause when we settle on definitions of religion that focus primarily as an institution with a set system of beliefs. A brief glimpse at most introductions to American religions syllabi reveals subjects such as "Native American religions," "Roman Catholicism," "Judaism," and "Evangelicalism." These terms have the appearance of traditions, and they certainly are that. And the leaders of these traditions appear in the classroom. When we study Puritans, we discuss Calvinism and introduce students to John Winthrop's writings. Class periods on Judaism engage the works of Isaac Mayer Wise and the founding documents of Reform Judaism. But our discussions of American religions should not begin and end with these foci. Likewise, our class examinations of religion definitions should not begin and end with lists of competing descriptions, but should go further to critically ask what kinds of work definitions do in making some ways of seeing the world seem natural and others never even up for discussion. The process of ordering the messiness of what scholars and practitioners describe as *religion* by narrowing it to being primarily a *belief system* conceals more than it reveals.

2

"Religions are intrinsically violent"

Matt Sheedy

On September 26, 2014, comedian Bill Maher unleashed a mini-firestorm on social media for comments he made on his program *Real Time with Bill Maher* about political correctness in the West and the apparent unwillingness of liberals to critique the rise of "radical Islam":

> If vast numbers of Muslims across the world believe, and they do, that humans deserve to die for merely holding a different idea or drawing a cartoon or writing a book or eloping with the wrong person, not only does the Muslim world have something in common with ISIS, it has too much in common with ISIS.[1]

The following week's episode of *Real Time* garnered even more attention for a heated debate between Maher and two of his guests, actor Ben Affleck and "New Atheist" Sam Harris, along with Michael Steele and Nicolas Kristof. Maher began the discussion by stating that "[l]iberals need to stand up for liberal principles," such as freedom of speech and belief, freedom to leave a religion, equality for women, and equality for minorities, including homosexuals, and claimed that most liberals hold a double-standard when it comes to critiquing the "Muslim world." This opened up the conversation to a variety of points and counterpoints, some of which are summarized below:

- "Islam at this moment is the mother-load of bad ideas." (Harris)

- That's racist. (Affleck)

- No it isn't. It is not (Muslim) people we are condemning, but their ideas. (Harris)

- "And people who believe in those ideas." (Maher)

- A basic liberal principle is tolerance. (Kristof)

- "But not for intolerance!" (Maher)

- There are many Muslims who aren't fanatics or jihadis, such as Malala Yousafzai. (Kristof)

- You (i.e., Maher and Harris) focus on a few bad things and generalize to the "whole religion." (Affleck)

- Ninety percent of Egyptians say that death is the appropriate response to leaving the religion. (Maher)

- The real divide is between fundamentalists and moderates in each faith. (Kristof)

- Moderate Muslim voices that speak out are rarely heard. (Steele)

- "There are hundreds of millions of nominal Muslims who don't take the faith seriously" and they should be propped-up as reformers of the faith. (Harris)[2]

The first thing to notice in this exchange is that all participants take for granted the idea that secular liberalism is an ideal to be followed and use it as a standard for evaluating those who are identified as Muslim. Whereas Maher and Harris, who both identify as atheists, claim that all religions are inherently irrational (and hence prone to violence) and that Islam is the worst among them, Affleck, Kristof, and Steele make a distinction between the majority of "moderate" Muslims and those who are extremist or "fundamentalist." In this example, we find several common assumptions that lie behind the cliché that religions are intrinsically violent, as well as the counterclaim that religions (or at least most religious people) are inherently peaceful. What these views share in common is the idea that religion is the primary lens through which we can understand certain groups of people, where religious identity is separated from other domains of social life, such as culture, ethnicity, politics, and so forth.

In what follows, I will examine the cliché that religions are intrinsically violent by first turning to some historical examples of how it has appeared in the past and in scholarly literature leading up to the present. Here I will argue that the claim that *all* religions are intrinsically violent is a relatively new one, since most scholars in the past presented a hierarchy of religions based on their presumed rationality, which included ideas about language and race. It is only with certain self-proclaimed atheists that we find the cliché that *all* religions are irrational and violent, though even here there are inconsistencies as will be discussed in due course. I will also turn briefly to look at the cliché that religions are intrinsically peaceful, as it reflects the same type of logic and is based on a similar understanding of religion. Finally, I will look at a few popular examples in which contemporary atheists have modified their earlier claims and now suggest, like earlier scholars of religion, that some religions are more rational and civilized than others. Guiding my argument throughout is an assumption that "religion" is a changing and unstable category that has no definitive meaning. As such, my ultimate interest will be in moving away from the question of what religion *means* or what it *is* and, instead, focus on how the term functions and what it *does* in different historical and social situations.

Some brief historical background

Unpacking the cliché that religions are intrinsically violent requires some brief discussion on the classification of the term religion and its relation to the term secular. The reason for this is fairly straightforward: without an understanding of religion as a category that is distinct and separate from other domains of social life, such as politics and economics, the cliché would make little sense. Scholars like Talal Asad (1993, 2003), Timothy Fitzgerald (2003,

2007), and Saba Mahmood (2005, 2015) have been particularly influential in showing how modern definitions of religion arose in the wake of the Protestant Reformation, giving rise to legal concepts such as the separation of church and state and debates about what kind of practices (e.g., veiling and polygamy) should be permitted, accommodated, or made illegal under "secular" law. At least two important points come from these critical studies. First, what is considered religion or secular cannot be reduced to a consistent or stable set of features in all cultures, times, and places. For example, standard classifications that understand religion "as being private, voluntary, individual, textual, and believed" (Sullivan 2007, 8) reflect modern political forms of social organization that were deeply influenced by Protestant Christianity and subsequently imposed throughout much of the world through colonization (see Smith 2004). From this it follows, second, that any analysis of what is conventionally termed "religion" must take into account the history of how these categories have been formed, and how they have been used for particular purposes. In most cases, what is deemed proper or acceptable religion will reflect the preferences and cultural background of dominant groups and the social norms that they wish to uphold in a particular time and place. In our present day, secular liberalism tends to be the standard by which all other nations, cultures, and religions are compared and, thus, warrants our attention for the discourses it creates, always including and excluding certain people, histories, and ideologies in the process.

Contemporary scholars of religion generally avoid the cliché that religions are intrinsically violent, although some do argue for its opposite, that religions are intrinsically peaceful (to be discussed later). Despite this current trend, however, there is a long history of Euro-Western scholarship arguing that *certain* religions are more prone to violence than *others*. In most cases prior to the mid-twentieth century, the religion or religions under discussion were also categorized along the lines of race or ethnicity, culture or custom, nation, empire, civilization, and so forth. Until recently, in fact, ideas of racial inferiority were commonplace in characterizations of non-Christian groups (see Alsultany 2012, Lewis 1990, Shaheen 2014), as well as with certain types of Christians, as seen with Protestant stereotypes about Catholics in places like England and the United States (Saunders 2012). The current Euro-Western emphasis on religious belief to characterize the behavior of a particular group or nation (especially Muslims) tends to exclude the category of race, which is due in large part to the influence of secular liberal ideology and its emphasis on things like tolerance and equal rights as guiding principles. This emphasis on tolerance and rights tends to exclude more critical examinations of systemic discrimination (e.g., racial, gendered, sexual) and the role that colonialism, imperialism, and neoliberal capitalism continues to play in social conflicts around the globe (see Brown 2006). Whatever else we might say about the category "religion," it should be noted that these other markers of identity are always tangled up within it.

There are numerous historical examples of Euro-Western scholars attempting to classify religions as more and less rational (and hence prone to violence or peace) from the sixteenth century onward, when increased contact with a variety of cultures through colonialism and, later on, increased efforts at translating sacred scriptures into European languages (mainly German, French, and English) led to a cottage industry of theorists opining on the nature and order of the "world religions."[3] One idea that animated this trend is what Edward Said famously termed "Orientalism" (1979), referring to the long history of Western representations of the "Orient" as the opposite or "Other" of Euro-Christian civilization. As Zachary Lockman argues in *Contending Visions of the Middle East* (2004), Orientalism relied heavily on the idea that the world was comprised of competing civilizations. Since this field of scholarship grew out of philology (a somewhat antiquated term for the comparative study of languages), there was an assumption that everything one needed to know about a so-called civilization could be found in its most sacred scriptures, written in languages that supposedly captured the essence of the civilization (e.g., Semitic, Aryan, etc.). In her book *The Invention of World Religions* (2005), Tomoko Masuzawa picks up on several of these arguments to show how early Orientalists viewed Islam as an inherently violent religion. As one example, she cites German theologian Otto Pfleiderer who writes:

The fundamental dogma [of] Islam is that of the unity of God; but concerning the nature of God, Mohammed made no deeper reflections. He conceived God as the supermundane, almighty ruler, similar to an Oriental despot; terrible in his anger and then again benevolent, delaying judgment in his benevolence, arbitrary in reward and punishment ... demanding blind submission of men and even then his grace uncertain. (Quoted in Masuzawa 2005, 200)

Here we see an early example of the idea that Islam—and by extension Muslims—can be understood by turning to what is written in the Qur'an, which is drawn on as primary evidence of the backward character of so-called Orientals. This idea is foundational for the cliché as it helps support the notion that Protestantism led to more rational and secular forms of government by permitting people the freedom to interpret sacred texts in whatever way they please, which eventually led to increased toleration and a recognition of secular authority as the only legitimate form of political order and law (Massad 2015). The point here, it should be stressed, is not to suggest that freedom of belief is a bad thing, but rather to highlight how privileging the Protestant model over all others has had the effect of obscuring the cultures, contexts, and identities of nondominant groups (e.g., Catholics, Muslims, Jews) in favor of caricatures and in creating an expectation that *they* conform to *our* rules of the game. In this way, the claim that particular religions are intrinsically violent works to characterize certain groups as irrational and thus in need of intervention, while masking other material interests, such as the maintenance of racial hierarchies and conflicts over land and resources (see Fernando 2014).

The less common claim that *all* religions are intrinsically violent is typically associated with atheist identities, which in our present day tends to signal an opposition to "organized religion" and a rejection of the belief in gods and the authority of scripture (see Quillen 2015). While this cliché is certainly not held by all atheists, it does not take much guesswork to see the advantage it holds for some who identify themselves this way since it lends support to atheism as an alternative or correct worldview. In this sense, the shift from condemning *some* to *all* religions as intrinsically irrational and violent is tied to a concern with the influence of theological ideas in the domains of scientific reasoning and modern secular forms of ethics (e.g., in debates over the teaching of evolution, sexual norms, and abortion). Following this logic, a just and rational world can only be achieved once religious ideas are abolished or at least weakened to the point where they hold no sway in the public-political domain.

One final example that illustrates the link between contemporary uses of the cliché, atheism, and the selective privileging of some religions over others comes from the Indian-British novelist Salman Rushdie. In his short essay, "'Imagine There's No Heaven': A Letter to the Six Billionth World Citizen," Rushdie (2007) evokes the famous musician John Lennon, who's song "Imagine" offers as clear an example of the cliché as one is likely to find, especially the following lines: "Nothing to kill or die for/And no religion too/Imagine all the people living life in peace." Addressing the world's six billionth citizen, Rushdie's letter cautions her to not be duped by the idea of some invisible Being in the sky that dictates morality and controls the natural order of things while urging her to embrace scientific and ethical reason. For Rushdie, it is only "blind faith" that perpetuates such "modern nonsenses," leading to things like a strict and harmful sexual morality and endless war. In one passage he writes:

> The real wars of religion, I have argued, are the wars religions unleash against ordinary citizens within their "sphere of influence." They are wars of the godly against the largely defenseless: American fundamentalists against pro-choice doctors, Iranian mullahs against their country's Jewish minority, the Taliban against the people of Afghanistan, Hindu fundamentalists in Bombay against that city's increasingly fearful Muslims. (Rushdie 2007, 382)

Although Rushdie appears to offer a balanced perspective here by pointing to a number of "religious" actors waging strife in local contexts, his examples fail to account for the multiple reasons why such conflicts might arise, such as ethnic differences, or the role that political and economic forces play in heightening tensions between certain groups, where religious identity is one among many sources of friction. For example, the role of the United States in arming and training Mujahideen fighters, including Osama bin Laden, during the Soviet-Afghan War (1979–89), which gave rise to the Taliban government and Al Qaeda, is excluded from Rushdie's analysis (see Mamdani 2004, Kumar 2012). By selectively privileging religious identity over all other variables, the reader is left with the impression that these conflicts are the result of superstitious ideas rather than a complex mix of multiple factors that include—but are not limited to—the influence of political theologies. In the process, a "secular-ethical position" is upheld as the best medicine for stamping out such antiquated views and is used to justify violence carried out by so-called secular states (see Cavanaugh 2009). Despite any claims that Rushdie or others might make to the contrary, his argument fails to account for *all* religions (as they are commonly defined) and focuses instead on a limited number of conflicts that are *framed in religious terms*—that is, they ignore other possible causes of conflict, such as competing military or nationalist interests. In this example, claiming that *all* religions are intrinsically violent says little about the complex and varied ideas that motivate violent actions and works instead to draw a line in the sand between so-called civilized nations (or groups within nations) from those who are deemed irrational or "barbaric" because they are too "religious." In the final section we will look at how a few contemporary atheists continue to push this argument, while admitting, in the face of much criticism, that religious identities are not as simple as they had once maintained, thus revealing another important dimension of the cliché: the claim that *all* religions are intrinsically violent is a rhetorical move that allows critics to appear neutral while calling out specific groups for special condemnation.

Religions are intrinsically peaceful clichés

I have yet to hear any contemporary scholar of religious studies make the claim that religions are intrinsically violent, though some in the recent past have used the term "cult" to distinguish violent groups, such as the Peoples Temple in Jonestown, from "authentic" religion (see Smith 1982). Part of the reason for this can be attributed to another common facet of the Protestant model, which holds that all religions, at their core, are ultimately about tolerance and a personal, spiritual quest for meaning. This can be seen in popular works on religion such as the writings of Karen Armstrong, a former British nun turned comparative religions historian, whose books have made it onto several bestsellers lists. In her book, *Islam: A Short History* (2002), for example, Armstrong provides a definition of religion that reflects several elements noted in the previous section:

> [The] spiritual quest is an interior journey; it is a psychic rather than a political drama. It is preoccupied with liturgy, doctrine, contemplative disciplines and an exploration of the heart, not with the clash of current events ... [P]ower struggles are not what religion is really about, but an unworthy distraction from the life of the spirit. (xi)

These ideas recall Sullivan's definition of the Protestant model cited in the previous section, especially the notion that proper religion is a private and individual affair based on personal beliefs. The idea that religions are intrinsically peaceful follows from this definition since it assumes that any engagement in the messy world of politics will corrupt the "true" meaning of religion. This idea can also be found in common descriptions of religious figures as embodiments of truth, as seen with John Locke's depiction of Jesus as "the prince of peace" in his famous "Letter Concerning Toleration," as well as common portrayals of the Prophet Muhammad. One example of the latter comes from the European scholar of Islamic Religious Studies at Oxford University, Tariq Ramadan, whose books have received a large readership around the world. In his book, *In the Footsteps of the Prophet* (2009), Ramadan remarks:

> Because Muhammad's life expressed the manifested and experienced essence of Islam's message, getting to know the Prophet is a privileged means of acceding to the spiritual universe of Islam. From his birth to his death, the Messenger's experience—devoid of any human tragic dimension—allies the call of faith, trail among people, humility, and the quest for peace with the One. (7)

It should be stressed here that the attempt to idealize certain figures like Jesus or Muhammad is perfectly fine as a theological aim, though when this is done in the form of scholarship, it lends academic credence to the same type of binary logic (religion = violence/peace) that we find in the cliché that religions are intrinsically violent. In this case, instead of suggesting that some or all religions are intrinsically violent, this other side of the binary presents a modern liberal reading of scripture that explains cruel or violent passages as either appropriate at the time they were written or, more commonly, as containing a deeper and metaphorical meaning that can be discovered with the correct interpretation. Like those who claim religions are violent, proponents of the peace cliché also tend to separate religion from politics, economics, and culture and emphasize their own preferred reading of scripture as the key to understanding the beliefs, practices, and motivations of those who are deemed "religious."

Thus far I have focused my attention on a few historical and contemporary examples of the cliché to provide some background on how modern conceptions of religion condition the boundaries of what gets called to our attention as either "religious" or "secular" in the first place. I have also noted how scholars have relied on a Protestant model, which emphasizes the role of belief in scripture, to carve out a special place for certain religions as more "rational" and "civilized" than others. Paying attention to these underlying ideological assumptions reveals that it is not "religion" that most proponents of the cliché object to—however we may define it—but a particular type of religious identity, while minimizing or excluding political, economic, and cultural factors, such as ethnicity and nationalism, from their analysis. In addition, I have argued that it is mainly with those who profess an atheist identity that we find a tendency to condemn *all* religions as intrinsically violent, which hinges on the idea that religion promotes irrational and childish behavior and inhibits modern forms of ethics and scientific reason. Even here, however, it is clear that proponents of this view draw on examples from a limited number of so-called religions to make their case and often modify their position when pressed with distinctions such "moderates" versus "fundamentalists," as seen with the example from *Real Time with Bill Maher*. This rhetorical move, it will be argued, continues to privilege religious identity above all else, while relying on secular liberal values as the measuring stick for what are deemed acceptable religious beliefs and practices.

Some examples of the cliché in popular culture

In the wake of the September 11, 2001, attacks, popular authors such as Richard Dawkins, Sam Harris, Christopher Hitchens, and Ayaan Hirsi Ali wrote best-selling books advocating for the abolition of religion, with subtitles such as "the end of faith" and "how religion poisons everything" driving this point home. Commonly referred to as "New Atheist," these authors have all gained an international reputation for their promotion of atheism and for their scathing critiques of religion, with particular attention paid to Christianity and Islam. A quick glance at some of their books, however, reveals the selective nature of their critiques, as well as wide variations on how they classify religion.

In the most popular books by Dawkins (2006), Harris (2004), and Hitchens (2007), only a handful of the so-called world religions are even mentioned, with Indigenous traditions, Shinto, Sikhism, and Taoism not even warranting an entry in the index. For example, in Dawkins best-selling book, *The God Delusion*, there is only a brief mention of Buddhism and Confucianism, which he classifies as more like "ethical systems or philosophes of life" than religions (Dawkins 2006, 38). Dawkins also characterizes Hinduism as "monotheism in disguise" (33), which allows him to lump it in with Judaism, Christianity, and Islam as the most virulent strains of the "God delusion." It is worth noting that Hindu beliefs, practices, and texts are not discussed anywhere in his book, though he does characterize riots between "Hindus" and "Muslims" in India as being religiously motivated (260). Harris and Hitchens also briefly address "Hindu" and "Muslim" violence in India and claim that religion is the underlying cause in the conflict over the disputed region of Kashmir. At one point, Hitchens suggests that Hinduism contains injunctions toward apocalyptic violence, citing Robert Oppenheimer's alleged reference to the *Bhagavad Gita*—"I am become Death, the destroyer of worlds"—as he watched the first nuclear test in New Mexico in 1945 (quoted in Hitchens 2007, 57). In this instance, one Westerner's remark is presented as evidence of the text's true or authentic meaning, despite the variety of uses to which it has been put. Harris and Hitchens also hold competing views on Buddhism. For Harris,

Buddhism and what he calls the "wisdom of the East" help people liberate themselves from "the illusion of the self," which he claims has no equivalent in the West (Harris 2004, 215). This reading not only reproduces Orientalist stereotypes about the "mystic East" as being more "spiritual" than the West (King 1999) but also ignores the ways in which such views are Western appropriations of Buddhism and Hinduism and do not reflect the majority of those who identify with these traditions throughout Asia and much of the world (see Lau 2000, Singleton 2010). Hitchens, for his part, views "Eastern faith" as more or less the same as "Western religion," citing the example of "Imperial-Way Buddhism" that was popular in Japan during the World War II as proof that Buddhism is, in fact, a violent religion (Harris 2007, 200–4).

What these brief examples show is that even among liked-minded Western critics of religion, all of whom cite and endorse each other's work and consider themselves friends, there is no consensus on what, exactly, constitutes a religion. What we find instead are idiosyncratic readings that reflect their shared support for atheism and secular liberalism, while presenting wide variations on what counts as religion, philosophy, and spirituality. In all cases, their main interest appears to be a rejection of the influence of (conservative) Christianity on the cultures that they grew up in and of speaking out against Islam as the number one threat to secular liberal values in the world today.

As the popularity of these authors grew and they began to appear as regular fixtures on talk shows and in the mainstream media, some critics began to point out how their depictions of religion reflected mostly conservative or literalist interpretations of scripture and did not account for moderate religious folk that supposedly make up the majority in every religion.[4] Initially, this critique caused some of these authors to double down, arguing that moderate religion provides cover for more "fundamentalist" interpretations of scripture by cherry-picking those passages it likes while ignoring others. In one example from *Letter to a Christian Nation* (2006), Harris characterizes religious moderates as follows:

> Another problem with religious moderation is that it represents precisely the sort of thinking that will prevent a rational and nondenominational spirituality from ever emerging in our

world. . . . What we need is a discourse about ethics and spiritual experience that is as unconstrained by ancient ignorance as the discourse of science already is. Science really does transcend the vagaries of culture. (106)

Much like Rushdie's argument in the previous section, "religion" is imagined here as intrinsically backward, no matter what interpretations or practices it may produce, since it inhibits moral and scientific reason through the continued promotion of antiquated beliefs. Underlying Harris's argument is an interest in promoting his own scientific interpretation of morality, which he does in *The Moral Landscape: How Science Can Determine Human Values* (2011), as well as a new type of "spirituality," which he argues for in *Waking Up: A Guide to Spirituality without Religion* (2014). Despite these earlier claims, Harris has modified his position in recent years in ways that more closely resemble the earlier Protestant and Orientalist ideas discussed in the previous section.

Perhaps the best example of Harris's shifting position can be seen in what he calls his "concentric circle" model of global Islam, which he lays out in his most recent book, co-authored with Maajid Nawaz, *Islam and the Future of Tolerance: A Dialogue* (2015). According to Harris,

[a]t the center are groups like the Islamic State, al-Qaeda, al-Shebab, Boko Haram, and so on. Their members apparently wake up each morning yearning to kill infidels and apostates. . . . Most of us refer to these people as "jihadists." Then there is a larger circle of Islamists who are more politically motivated and appear less eager to kill and be killed. Beyond that is a wider circle of Muslims who probably support jihad and Islamism . . . but are not inclined to get their hands dirty. Finally, one hopes, there is a much larger circle of so-called moderate Muslims . . . who want to live by more modern values. Although they may not be quite secular, they don't think that groups like the Islamic State represent their faith. Perhaps there are also millions of truly secular Muslims who just don't have a voice. (151)

This marks a significant change in Harris's thinking, as it allows him to form alliances with public figures like Maajid Nawaz, and to concede the point, made by Nawaz and others, that holding a religious identity does not prohibit a commitment to science or secularism. Nevertheless, the underlying logic of Harris's approach remains basically unchanged. Violence committed at the hands of those who claim (or are labeled with) an Islamic (or religious) identity is understood to be the result of religious beliefs, especially the idea of jihad. Those who identify as Muslim but do not subscribe to such beliefs have apparently been influenced enough by "modern values" to not take their religion too seriously, and it is these people that Harris wants to enlist in his cause. This modified position continues to follow the premise that religion guides people's beliefs and practices, while subordinating political, economic, and cultural variables, or ignoring them altogether. In addition, the speculation that there are perhaps millions of "truly secular Muslims" is not only wishful thinking on Harris's part but also a subtle claim to the power of secularism and its universal appeal. A similar argument can be found in the writings of Ayaan Hirsi Ali, who is unique among the "New Atheist" for having been raised Muslim and for focusing the majority of her critiques on Islam.

Raised a devout Muslim in Somalia, Saudi Arabia, Ethiopia, and Kenya, Hirsi Ali applied for political asylum in Holland at the age of twenty-three, where she received a university education in philosophy and eventually served in the Dutch Parliament. She would later immigrate to the United States after the murder of Theo van Gogh, with whom she codirected a short documentary critical of Islam called *Submission*. Hirsi Ali recounts her experiences as a youth in *The Caged Virgin* (2008a), including undergoing genital cutting; her transition away from Islam in *Infidel* (2008b); her migration to the United States in *Nomad* (2011), where she urged moderate Muslims to convert to Christianity, a claim that she later retracted;[5] and *Heretic: Why Islam Needs a Reformation Now* (2015b), where she lays out the stakes of her argument as follows:

> My argument is that it is foolish to insist, as our leaders habitually do, that the violent acts of radical Islamists can be divorced from the religious ideals that inspire them. Instead we must acknowledge that they are driven by a political ideology, an ideology embedded in Islam itself, in the holy book of the Qur'an as well as the life and teachings of the Prophet Muhammad contained in the hadith. (65–70)

This line of argument touches on a number of themes that we have discussed so far, including the idea that religions are best understood as manifestations of scripture and that conflicts that involve religious identities are driven, first and foremost, by people's beliefs and not by material factors, such as war, poverty, ethnic strife, and so forth—a point that Hirsi Ali makes a little further on in her book in no uncertain terms: "Hard as it may be for many Western academics to believe, when people commit violent acts in the name of religion, they are not trying somehow to dignify their underlying socioecomonic or political grievances" (2015, 344). Hirsi Ali also rejects the idea that religions are intrinsically peaceful by claiming that it is wrong to separate "religious ideals" from the violent actions of "radical Islamists." While we can certainly agree with this statement, given the theoretical approach toward religion that was laid out in the introduction of this chapter, Hirsi Ali merely reproduces the other side of the cliché by claiming to know what the meaning of Islam *is* rather than focus on what it *does* and is *made to do* in different historical and social contexts of interaction.

Like Harris, Hirsi Ali has undergone a significant change in perspective in recent years, from calling for the abolition of religion, and advocating that Muslims convert to Christianity (because it is more compatible with secular values), to her current view that seeks to differentiate three types of Muslims. The first type is labeled "Medina Muslims," who she characterizes as follows: "They aim not just to obey Muhammad's teaching, but also to emulate his warlike conduct after his move to Medina. Even if they do not themselves engage in violence, they do not hesitate to condone it" (2015b, 234). Medina Muslims also advocate murdering infidels who refuse to convert to Islam, preach jihad, and promote death through martyrdom. They are said to represent about 3 percent of the world's Muslims, which is estimated at around 48 million people. The second type is labeled "Mecca Muslims," who comprise the majority of adherents around the world. They are said to be devout but not inclined toward violence, while still representing a serious problem since:

> their religious beliefs exist in an uneasy tension with modernity—
> the complex of economic, cultural, and political innovations
> that not only reshaped the Western world but also dramatically

transformed the developing world as the West exported it. The rational, secular, and individualistic values of modernity are fundamentally corrosive of traditional societies, especially based on gender, age, and inherited status. (246)

Mecca Muslims are preferable to Medina Muslims, though they are said to live in a constant state of "cognitive dissonance," forced to reconcile their beliefs with the imperatives of secular liberal societies that challenge them at every turn. This dissonance, she argues, is typically resolved in one of two ways: "either leave Islam altogether, as I did, or abandon the dull routine of daily observance for the uncompromising Islamic creed offered by those—the Medina Muslims—who explicitly reject the West's modernity" (2015b, 259). It is this latter group that Hirsi Ali wishes to engage in her book and to win over to her side. This leads to the third type, labeled "Modifying Muslims," which includes those who have left Islam but continue to debate its future and "reforming believers" who have sufficiently adapted to modernity in her eyes (273).

As with Harris's concentric circle model, Hirsi Ali's typology can be understood as a rhetorical strategy since it appears to account for complexity and purports to be "neutral," merely criticizing people's beliefs and ideas, as Bill Maher stated in the opening example in this chapter—be they Hindu, Muslim, or Christian—which is justified as a "liberal principle." This rhetorical move, as noted, foregrounds the alleged "beliefs" of certain groups in a conflict and characterizes them as irrational, which has the effect of minimizing cultural, political, and economic factors and of upholding secular liberalism as an ideal to be followed, while legitimizing violence carried out in its name.

Conclusion

To be clear, and in the interest of avoiding any confusion, it is not my intention to suggest that theological ideas do not have violent effects in the social world. To the contrary, many theologies derive their authority from ancient scriptural passages, some of which are violent and can be marshaled to justify acts of violence. The point that I would like to stress in closing is that, when it comes to religious identities, contests over interpretation are all that we have, which are shaped by local and historical contexts in myriad ways. Religious identities are never only "religious" but also nationalistic, ethnic, political, economic, cultural, and so forth. In this sense, "religion" cannot be anything, once and for all, since it depends on what counts as "religion" in a particular time and place and how such identities are shaped by the material world around them. Paying attention to what religious ideas and identities do and are made to do in different times and places, then, can tell us more about the role of theologies in creating, preventing, or enduring violence than any focus on some imaged set of beliefs ever will.

3

"Religion makes people moral"

Jennifer Eyl

In March 2015, Phil Robertson, the patriarch of the reality television show *Duck Dynasty*, illustrated a frightening hypothetical scenario in which two assailants enter the home of an atheist family and wreak havoc. While systematically murdering each family member, one of the hypothetical assailants says to the father of the family, "Isn't it great that I don't have to worry about being judged? Isn't it great that there's nothing wrong with this? There's no right or wrong, now is it, dude? [*sic*]" The other assailant says, "But you're the one who says there is no God, there's no right, there's no wrong, so we're just having fun. We're sick in the head, have a nice day." At the end of his bizarre story Phil Robertson claims, "If it happened to them, they probably would say, 'Something about this just ain't right.'" His portrayal of atheists is such that they can sort of tell right from wrong, but morality is an alien notion without God. The best an atheist family can muster, while being violated and murdered, is that *something* isn't acceptable about this, but they can't quite put their finger on it (Jancelewicz 2015). We see similar claims from a more theologically sophisticated perspective, as well. For example, in 2007, Reverend Al Sharpton and avowed atheist Christopher Hitchens debated the topic of religion at the New York Public Library. At one point Reverend Sharpton comments, "If there is no God and there is no supreme mechanism that governs the world, what makes right right and what makes wrong wrong? ...

There is no moral code because there is nobody to judge that"
(Sharpton and Hitchens 2007).

This essay will explore and critique the claim that religion
makes people moral. To do so, I will draw from scholars who work
in primatology, cognitive evolution, and theory of religion. The
two previous examples illustrate the common assumption that
without religion, humans lack a moral compass. Because we are
not equipped to formulate distinctions between right and wrong,
we would freely behave in ways that are unjust, cruel, deceitful,
and unethical, without the fear of divine judgment and punishment.
Lack of religion, and atheism in particular, then, is a rejection of
ethics and morality. At best, the human character is a blank slate
and God keeps us in check; at worst, human nature is deeply flawed
and gravitates toward evil, thus God is indispensable for our moral
choices. In some ways, these assumptions are incorrect, and in
other ways, they are more complicated than the stereotypes allow
for. Three significant observations challenge the claim: (1) most
religious practices and beliefs have little to do with morality and
ethics, (2) humans ubiquitously have notions of right and wrong,
regardless of whether they invoke gods, and (3) humans do both
"good" *and* "bad" things in the name of gods. In fact, members
of the same religion often disagree about what constitutes "right"
and "wrong." For example, some Christians believe it is immoral to
be gay or lesbian, while other equally devout Christians disagree
entirely. Indeed, many Christian clergy leaders are themselves gay
and lesbian. Thus, religion is intrinsically neither good nor bad but is
instrumental in cultivating (or, enforcing) specific types of behaviors
and practices, regardless of the moral value of such behaviors and
practices.

What is morality? What is religion?

What does it mean to be moral? What are ethics? For that matter,
what is religion? These questions are complex, and the answers
vary greatly, depending on who we ask: professional philosophers
and ethicists, politicians seeking a vote, soldiers engaged in war,
orthodox religious practitioners and theologians, contemporary
college students, and so on. The word "moral" itself derives from

the Latin *mos/moris* meaning "custom, principle, or law." The Roman philosopher/statesman Cicero links *mos* to ethics when he uses it as a Latin translation for the Greek word *ēthikos*. For some, strict obedience to set doctrine and rigid adherence to ritual is a demonstration of morality. For others, following the Golden Rule, which is found in many societies (*mutatis mutandis*), is a basic moral code. Still for others, morality and ethics come down to loyalty to the group, even in the face of certain death. Thus, part of the difficulty in addressing the cliché that "religion makes people moral" is being attentive to the diversity of opinions regarding what morality is. Colloquially, is "being moral" the same thing as "being a good person"? And if so, what constitutes "goodness"?

Sociologist Edward Westermarck argued that moral feelings go beyond one's immediate self-interest and extend to human behavior more generally. Thus, morality addresses the "ought" of human actions: How ought one act in a given situation? How ought one treat oneself and others? What is the difference between right and wrong? Primatology expert Frans de Waal observes, "It is only when we make general judgments of how anyone ought to be treated that we can begin to speak of moral approval and disapproval" (de Waal 2006, 20). De Waal has argued that the pillars of morality are compassion and reciprocity: "No moral society could be imagined without reciprocal exchange and an emotional interest in others" (21). Indeed, many contemporary ethicists agree with de Waal. Moral philosopher Richard Joyce writes, "The actions that morality prescribes with categorical force are those that constitute or promote, roughly speaking, cooperation" (Joyce 2000, 714; see also Joyce 2006). This is not to suggest that being uncooperative is immoral; one can imagine a number of scenarios in which cooperation with others might, in fact, be looked on as immoral or unethical. Yet, overall concern for the self and others constitutes the foundation of behavior that ethicists, philosophers, and everyday folks have traditionally categorized as "moral" or "ethical."

A second significant challenge to addressing the supposed link between religion and morality is that religion itself has no clear definition, and most languages do not even have a word for religion. This may strike the reader as surprising or strange, but the things modern westerners set apart and identify as "religious" are so deeply imbedded in and diffused throughout most cultures that they are not understood as a separate sphere of activity. The distinct categories of the "religious" and "secular" have been invented only in the past few hundred years (see Asad 2003, Nongbri 2013). For the purposes of this critique, however, I will use the term "religion" to refer to the diverse constellation of practices, discourses, and beliefs that in some way pertain to invisible beings (gods, demigods, ghosts, demons, spirits, saints, etc.). To be sure, this is an oversimplification of all those forms of culture we often label as religion, but keeping religion closely aligned with invisible/nonobvious beings allows for my critique of the religion-morality claim, because most people making such claims equate religion with belief in God(s).

Gods, morality, and cognitive evolution

Making claims about the relationship between gods and morality is hardly a modern development. Even ancient writers discussed the question and disagreed with one another. For example, in his lengthy treatise on ethics, the *Nicomachean Ethics*, Aristotle (384–322 BCE) barely mentions God or gods. While the cosmos may be the result of an ultimate and impersonal creator-deity—which he calls the Unmoved Mover in *Metaphysics*—Aristotle's ethics are anthropocentric (i.e., they are human-focused). When Aristotle speaks of "the divine," he is not speaking of a God or gods, but as a theoretical principle related to excellence, virtue, and the highest parts of the human character. Another Greek philosopher, Epicurus (341–270 BCE), argued that people could absolutely be moral without attendance to the gods. In fact, in Epicurean philosophy, the gods take no interest in human affairs, and humans only waste time and create undue suffering when they worry about what the gods might want or think. Instead, Epicurus and his followers espoused a strong ethic of mutual care between humans, devoid of all discussion of gods or religion (see, for instance, Epicurus' *Letter to Herodotus* and *Principle Doctrines*). Centuries after Aristotle and Epicurus, Augustine of Hippo (354–430 CE) introduced a theological concept that most iterations of Western Christianity have since inherited and reproduced: Original Sin.

According to Augustine's theory, all humans everywhere are born into a state of sinfulness due to the transgressions of Adam and Eve in Genesis 3. Augustine's ideas are rooted in his reading of a Latin mistranslation of Romans 5:12, yet his theory gained authority nonetheless. In his treatise, *On Grace and Free Will*, Augustine claims that human nature is flawed and incapable of doing good without the guiding grace of God.[1] In *Confessions*, Augustine reflects on innate human depravity, as evidenced by the selfish rage, jealousy, and competitiveness that infants feel while clamoring for a mother's breast milk. European Christian theologians after Augustine reinterpret his ideas but can never escape them as doctrine. John Calvin (1509–64) argues that humanity is so profoundly depraved, by nature, that even when a person appears to be doing good, she or he is not; only God can do good. Thus, a "good" person is actually a (bad) person channeling the goodness of God.

Despite what various philosophers and theologians have claimed over the centuries, a growing body of evidence by cognitive scientists and primatologists suggests that humans act compassionately and "morally" without the watchful eyes of a God or multiple gods.[2] This research points to our innate tendencies toward cooperation, empathy, sympathy, kindness, fairness, and other attributes we associate with being "good" or "moral." In fact, such researchers argue that there are clear evolutionary benefits for cooperation, empathy toward others, and attention to fairness and equality. These priorities result in what scholars call "prosocial" behaviors in primates, including humans. Prosocial behaviors strengthen group bonds, allow individuals to accomplish difficult tasks through cooperation, and promote things like sharing in times of dearth and protection for weaker members of the group. De Wahl's Prosocial Choice Test has demonstrated prosociality among chimpanzees, but we can see such behavior in YouTube videos regularly: elephants protecting members of the herd, dogs saving one another and/or their humans, and dolphins working together for a common goal. The Prosocial Choice Test, however, shows that some great apes will intentionally make choices that benefit other apes, with no advantage for the ape making the choice.[3] Human and nonhuman animals alike demonstrate care for and cooperation with others.

Furthermore, some cognitive scientists have argued that making moral judgments is an evolutionary adaptation (Fraser 2010).

Neuroscientist Marco Iacoboni (2009) has asserted that our capacity to feel the pain of others is hardwired in our neurons. While many have suggested that the human tendency toward imitation of others appears to be linked to our capacity for empathy, Iacoboni's study examines that link on a cognitive, neural level. Mirror neurons, as these neurons are called, fire in the brain when, for instance, we see the hand of another person driven through with a nail, causing us to flinch and retract our own hands. Likewise, they fire simply when we see another person execute a physical task, as we ourselves can imagine doing the same task with the same body parts (e.g., lifting a mug with our hands or kicking a ball with our feet). Such neurons are activated because "perception and action share common representational formats" in the mind (659). But what has this to do with morality? Mirror neurons are foundational constituents of prosocial behavior and generate a cognitive and emotional link between us as embodied creatures.[4] Similarly, without invoking the gaze of a deity, we feel disgust at egregious demonstrations of selfishness and greed, as in the case of Martin Shkreli. As the CEO of Turing Pharmaceuticals, Shkreli suddenly raised the price of the drug Daraprim by 5,000 percent in 2015. Overnight, he was dubbed America's Most Hated Man for price gouging the only drug available to treat toxoplasmosis (see O'Connell 2015, Herper 2016). Regardless of religious identification, the sentiment Americans most vehemently expressed regarding the Shkreli case was *moral outrage*.[5]

A note of caution here: I am not suggesting that humans, the world over, share the same moral codes, nor am I suggesting that the similarities existing between various moral expectations are inevitable or "natural." Any claims to the "naturalness" of social mores and moral codes are suspect to begin with, as the notion of "nature" is so often utilized to assert particular schemas of power, insofar as people take their own social mores and label them "natural" to make them appear legitimate to others. "Natural" renders invisible the arbitrariness of strategies that attempt to construct and maintain a status quo. What I am suggesting, instead, is that many of the building blocks of what ethicists call "morality" exist independently of gods/religion and can be found even among nonhuman primates.

Modes of religiosity

The majority of religious practices and discourses, crossculturally and transhistorically, do not pertain to ethics or morality. In fact, some scholars argue that the default mode of religiosity involves humans interacting with nonobvious beings (gods, spirits, ancestors, etc.) in ways that are quite similar to how we interact with other persons—except gods, spirits, and so forth have more power and knowledge. Most people across the globe and across time have petitioned gods to make their lives livable and safe; gods are not primarily petitioned to save the soul after death or to adjudicate moral quandaries. Gods themselves are often amoral or even *im*moral (one thinks of the chronic misbehavior of the Greek god Zeus, the Norse god Loki, or the Hindu god Krishna). Gods oversee the growing of crops, the birth of children, protection from harm, healing from diseases, the outcome of competitive events (wars,[6] elections [see Editorial staff 2010, Barrick 2012], the Superbowl[7]), and any other activities that humans participate in for which they want or need extra strength, protection, guidance, and/or insider information. The ascertaining of special insider information comes in the form of prayerful petitions and reading divine signs. Religion scholar Stanley Stowers refers to this default mode of religiosity as the "religion of everyday social exchange," in which gods are thought to have human-like psychologies and personalities, and mortals strive to maintain positive reciprocal relationships with them (Stowers 2011). These interactions are neither moral nor immoral, but rather, replicate the practical, commonsense know-how of being a social creature in the world: making food (shared with gods), talking (to gods), cutting one's hair (for gods), and any other mundane practice that is ritualized and in orientation to such invisible beings.

Anthropologist Harvey Whitehouse is an early proponent for thinking of religiosity in terms of "modes." For Whitehouse, modes of religiosity, "constitute attractor positions around which ritual actions and associated religious concepts cumulatively tend to cluster" (Whitehouse 2004, 74).[8] Thus, one mode of religiosity may involve the practical "how-type" knowledge of everyday social exchange (i.e., the appropriate methods for preparing food, talking, or cutting one's hair, as explored by Stanley Stowers), while another mode generates "why-type" knowledge of complex theological claims, doctrines, and theories about the cosmos, ethics, morals, and ultimate truths. When Whitehouse speaks of "attractor positions" he means that any ritual does not rigidly conform to one mode or another, but rather, tends toward one mode or the other. Thus, some practices and rituals capitalize on and cultivate memorable bodily responses and habits, whereas other rituals capitalize on and cultivate complicated cerebral activities (via the use of texts, metaphor, symbolism, paradox, etc.).

The "why-type" knowledge often makes great use of literacy, as the memory is taxed by complex, counterintuitive ideas and often includes the interpretation of texts. Examples of such complex, counterintuitive ideas include deliberations about the nature of the cosmic (and thus, divine) order and how that order pertains to ethics and philosophy.[9] For example, the Christian Trinity is a counterintuitive claim; the mind must bend to understand how "three" can simultaneously be "one." Furthermore, it is equally counterintuitive to suppose that one or all members of the three-in-one Trinity assess the complicated ethical choices made by all human beings, all of the time, all over the world, from Scranton to Shanghai. Such claims are so counterintuitive, in fact, that early Christian theologians battled one another via treatises, letters, and councils until one group of theologians (backed by the resources of the Roman Emperor Constantine) won pride of place. Their ideas were labeled "orthodoxy," and the numerous other theological claims were labeled "heresy." To this day, the results of early Christian intellectual debates are reinforced by Christians across the globe on Sundays in the prayer called the Apostle's Creed.

Modes of religiosity always go hand in hand with broader economic and social conditions, since the things that make up "religion" are themselves social practices. And since religion and morality are not synonymous (often lacking overlap at all), it is helpful to ask: When do they overlap? Under what social conditions do people bundle together ideas about gods with moral positions? Again, if we return to early Western history, we see that the overlapping of religious discourses and questions about morality/ethics took place in philosophy. Presocratic philosophers (Heraclitus, Thales, etc.) typically asked questions about how the natural world operated, but after Socrates (d. 399 BCE), philosophy often turned its attention to morality, ethics, and variations on the questions, What is the right way to live? What does it mean to be good? What is the source of human suffering? Plato, Chrysippus, Diogenes, and many others often tied these questions to ideas about God and the nature of the cosmos. In the *Timaeus*, Plato argues that the ultimate creator-deity (which he called *Demiourgos*, or Craftsman) constructs the cosmos, all other deities, and immortality itself. Those secondary deities (the Olympians, which most Greeks would have thought of as the primary deities) are tasked by the creator deity with mixing a portion of what is immortal with perishable materiality, thus creating immortal souls entombed in mortal human bodies. There is a direct link, according to Plato, between the moral and ethical choices of humans, and their souls after death: the weakest, most cowardly, and most immoral men are reincarnated as women.

Stoic philosophers devoted numerous treatises to viewing the cosmos, theology, and ethics in relation to one another: Cleanthes's *On the Gods*, Persaeus's *On Impiety*, Chrysippus's *On the Gods* and *On Zeus*, Seneca's *Natural Questions*, and many more. The apostle Paul, furthermore, takes up Greek philosophical discourse about morals and rewrites human history in his letter to the Romans to explain why Gentiles are dogged by ethical depravity. He argues that long ago, the people who turned their backs on the Judean creator-god were subsequently abandoned by him and fell into insurmountable moral deficiencies. These people became Gentiles and were enslaved to their immoral passions (lust, greed, anger, deceit, etc.; see Romans 1.18–32). Returning to the family of Abraham through the vehicle of Christ was the only answer for such profound depravity.

Plato, the Stoics, and moral-religious entrepreneurs like Paul link discourses about ethics and morality to ideas about gods, the cosmos, eternity, and one's condition in life (or, as the case may be, the afterlife). As we have seen, however, not everyone in antiquity would agree with these ideas: Epicurus, in particular, identified the human preoccupation with gods as the source of human suffering. The general population around philosophers certainly had traditional ideas about right and wrong, but the domain of philosophical discourse turned questions about ethics and morality into complex and elaborate codes of conduct and mental dispositions. Many early philosophers argued that the complex doctrines they promoted were the result of a divine order of an omniscient, omnipotent creator-deity. Such omniscience and omnipotence are characteristic of the type of super deities who often patrol the doings and sayings of people and stand as moral exemplars and lawgivers. Plato, for example, is deeply irritated by the fickle, humanlike personalities attributed to the gods in popular Greek religion. For him, God is sublime, moral, and perfect. Paul denies that the gods of popular Greek religion are legitimate gods at all—they are more like *daimones* (low-level deities whom Christians will later refer to as demons).

It is important to note that complex questions about ethics and morality have typically been undertaken primarily in philosophy and not "religion." But because of the prominence of intellectual, literate, Christian theologians (who are, effectively, Christian philosophers), we have inherited centuries of philosophical discourse that often links moral questions to a cosmic divine order, resulting (for modern westerners) in the mistaken notion that "religion" and "morality" are innately linked. Thus, the "why-type" mode of religiosity yokes morality to religion, though that connection is simply the result of certain intellectual practices and interests. This is best exemplified by the perplexity that many westerners have regarding how to categorize Buddhism—is it a philosophy or a religion? The question itself underscores our implicit cultural understanding that ethics and philosophy "go together" but also, sometimes, ethics and religion "go together" too.

Behaving badly with God on your side

As often as people explain their kindnesses, virtues, and compassion through their religious beliefs and practices, people likewise do terrible things in the name of gods. By "terrible things" I mean that gods, religion, and religious teachings are often cited as the justification for social practices that many others deem horrifying and immoral. In the name of specific types of Christianity, abortion clinics in the United States are occasionally bombed. In the name of Allah, radical Islamic suicide bombers kill scores of innocent bystanders. Nineteenth-century white American slave owners justified the brutality of slavery by pointing to its centrality in the

Bible. In the aftermath of the Emancipation Proclamation, the Ku Klux Klan introduced cross burnings as a Christian ritual in which the light of (white) Jesus shines through the darkness of the world. The wall between Israel and Palestine, which detractors liken to Israel's version of South African Apartheid, is often justified by claiming that God gave that land to Israelites—the modern inheritance of a covenantal land grant found repeatedly in Torah. A similar large-scale "land grant that involves the involuntary mass displacement of others" appears in American history in the form of Manifest Destiny. A term first used in 1845, Manifest Destiny asserted that the spread of white, European, Christian domination of the North American continent was part of God's plan for humanity (see Weeks 1996).[10] Centuries prior to Manifest Destiny, Christopher Columbus believed himself to be chosen by God to find a trade route to the East, thereby securing the funds for another Christian Crusade (see Delaney 2012). Now in the early twenty-first century, Columbus' violent extermination of the people he encountered in the Caribbean has generated widespread condemnation and the renaming of Columbus Day.

I point to the controversial examples above to demonstrate the intricate relationship between religion and morality. This is more complex than the adage, "one man's terrorist is another man's freedom fighter." As often as religious practices, beliefs, and institutions contribute to charities and hospitals, broker peace accords, and assert human rights (which de Waal would call "prosocial" activities), so humans also draw on religious discourses to bolster themselves in political conflict, justify sexualized or racialized violence, and maintain severely hierarchical social structures that put specific demographics (based on sex, race, geography, etc.) at an insurmountable disadvantage. Because we currently live in an age in which the rhetoric of equality has currency, external forces that generate an insurmountable disadvantage are viewed as wrong and immoral.

In all of the aforementioned examples, one notices that religious ideology masks, and is coterminous with, other interests: sexual domination, capitalizing on free human labor, a vehement land grab, resistance to imperialism, the claiming of natural resources (water, oil, precious metals, timber, etc.), and political power. Religious interests are never separate from these other interests, because what we call "religion" is not, in fact, a separate or unique sphere of human activity. People who do "bad things" with God(s) on their side are not doing religion "wrongly" since religion is neither more nor less moral than any other type of human activity. Competition over authority, negotiations of power, identity formation, ideologies, and all other types of human activities that make up society are also the constituent features of what we call religion.

Big gods and surveillance

If religion is not necessarily a question of morality, then why do people like Phil Robertson and Al Sharpton claim that, without God, people will act freely in any way they choose? Is there a connection between invoking gods and ensuring that people may act in one way or another? The answer to that appears to be yes—the threat of divine justice can be used to police and control people. We have innumerable examples of this. The second century Christian text, *Apocalypse of Peter*, for example, provides a detailed description of an early Christian version of hell. A disproportionate number of "sins" punished in this graphic, gruesome place of torment are practices of sexuality and speech; adulterers hang for eternity by their genitals, while liars and blasphemers hang by their tongues. The public cannot always trace an evil rumor to its source; a husband does not always know if his wife (and thus, property, by ancient Mediterranean standards) is having an affair. Unacceptable sexual and speech practices cannot always be discovered and punished, but God sees all, and God punishes all. Thus, the gaze of a god coupled with descriptions of hell can act as a sort of Foucauldian panopticon, causing people to police themselves.[11] Classic Christian texts such as Dante's *Inferno* and the sermons of Jonathan Edwards operate in much the same way.

Let us return for a moment to the issue of reciprocity. In Frans de Waal's Prosocial Choice Test, the chimpanzees involved were not random; they knew one another and lived together. While not related genetically, they shared the same social group and thus shared and maintained ongoing relations of reciprocity. In larger-scale human societies, which have developed only in the last 10,000 years, humans have often lived in proximity to one another without always being genetically related or part of a tightly bounded social group. Ara Norenzayan argues for a correlation between large-scale societies, in which anonymity is common and the ties of kinship do not reinforce prosocial behavior, and what he calls Big Gods—the types of gods who police, monitor, reinforce behaviors, and construct groupness that the immediate kin group cannot do on such a large scale (see Norenzayan 2013). Although Norenzayan utilizes the problematic category *natural religion*, his overall study points to the usefulness of omniscient deities capable of large-scale surveillance and punishment/reward when people are not beholden to predictable, delineated codes of behavior toward others.[12]

I would add, however, that Big Gods are not the only entities that accomplish similar goals; such watchful eyes come in the form of "small gods" like Elf on the Shelf, Mensch on the Bench, and Santa Claus (particularly for children in the United States). Furthermore, as technologies of state surveillance become more ubiquitous and sophisticated, the surveillance skills of a big or small god become less important. Some scholars have argued that "children's gods" like Mensch on the Bench and Elf on the Shelf prime young people to lead lives complicit with state surveillance (even though their intended use for parents is to train children to self-regulate).[13] However, the surveillance role of strongmen gods is simply replaced by the state (and/or anonymous citizens) when it steps in to monitor subjects. One does not need to worry about divine retribution for lying under oath if there is a cell phone video recording to prove that the person on trial did (or did not) commit the crime in question. In that sense, the roles of Santa Claus, Elf on the Shelf, and Mensch on the Bench equally condition young children to live as subjects monitored by the state *and* by God(s).[14]

Conclusion

In conclusion, there are three significant reasons why religion is not necessarily a force in making people moral: (1) humans have a sense of right and wrong that exists independently from our beliefs and practices about gods or divine punishment, (2) most religious practices do not pertain to morality or ethics, and (3) just as often as humans act morally and attribute their "goodness" to religion, they likewise act "immorally" in the name of gods and/or religion. Thus, the connection between morality and religion is not inevitable or consistent. However, religion *can* play a role in moral discourse and moral behavior in two major ways that should not be overlooked: (1) some modes of religiosity expand and enrich our default tendencies toward prosociality by constructing complex teachings on moral behavior (such as the *Tao Te Ching*, Gospel of Matthew, or the Buddhist Silas), and (2) invoking the watchful eyes of a deity can prompt people to monitor their own behavior and conform to the moral code to which they sense they should adhere. The specifics of these moral codes are socially constructed and vary from place to place and over time.

4

"Religion concerns the transcendent"

Leslie Dorrough Smith

After suffering for several weeks from a bout of insomnia that left me feeling perpetually groggy, I found myself explaining my plight in a way that I thought was rather obvious: I needed rest. Because I thought of my body as something like a motor that must stop periodically lest it overheats, I was convinced that sleep allowed all but my most vital bodily functions to shut down so that I could be competent several hours later. If anything, isn't "rest" precisely the essence of what sleep is, after all?

In the midst of this insomniac episode, I came across an interesting podcast from a show called *RadioLab*, which is well-known for unearthing the scientific sides of what seem to be relatively mundane topics. One episode in particular, on the topic of sleep, showed that my own perceptions about sleep are relatively inaccurate (Krulwich and Abumrad 2013). Despite the fact that I perceive sleep to be about resting or ceasing to function in some way, the show's interviews with cutting edge neurologists indicate just the opposite: although sleep is not fully understood, what is clear is that it is a rather active neurological process that does not imply a cessation in function at all. As it turns out, many animals sleep in a perpetually alert state so as to guard against predators or to make sure respiration occurs for those that must consciously breathe (like dolphins). For humans, the process of sleep serves a critical organizational function that makes possible both learning and memory. Sleep, it turns out, is far more than "just rest."

I tell this little story because it seems to me that our perceptions of religion function in much the same way: there are some things about religion that virtually everyone seems to take for granted—ideas that are so widespread that no one seems to really question them. But with a closer look, those of us interested in examining the social patterns associated with religion might find a completely different set of phenomena at work that are indicative of far more than what appearances might suggest.

This is the case with one of the most beloved, long-standing, and—arguably—unverifiable claims most commonly made about religion, which is that it is fundamentally about some sort of engagement with a transcendent force or power. While the term "transcendent" is probably not the first adjective that the average person might think of when describing religion, the meaning behind it is quite commonly used, for it implies something above and beyond the normal human experience. Thus, when we hear people say that religion is about a "higher power," or a relationship with "the sacred" or "the divine," they are referring to the concept of transcendence, for all of these phrases point to a force that is somehow fundamentally different from or stands outside of the ordinary world.

For those of us interested in the ways in which critical thought can help us see the often hidden patterns of social life, what makes this situation particularly intriguing is the authority given to an invisible entity. Consider the fact that, if I am an entymologist (a scientist who studies insects), then my work revolves around the fact that there are tangible things called insects to study. If, however, I claim to be a scientist who studies zombies (a zombologist?), I am unlikely to hold the same authority as an entymologist because what I claim to study does not exist except in people's imaginations.

There are very few (if any) other fields of academic inquiry where one would be able to study a subject of which no one can verify the existence in some sort of objective way, and yet in the field of religion, scholarship presuming (or at least not questioning) the existence of "the transcendent" or "the sacred" is created all of the time. Whether or not such beings or essences really exist (even if such proofs are beyond scientific reasoning) is not the issue I seek to address here, for my interest, instead, lies in thinking about how we very readily tolerate this logical inconsistency because of the social effects that are achieved when we engage it.

Using that approach, this chapter will consider the longevity and utility of the cliché that the central feature of religion is that it is a human relationship with a transcendent or divine power. We will examine the idea through examples from both pop culture and academic scholarship to look at some important ways that it has been deployed and thus popularized. Although the use of the transcendence concept differs depending on the context, time, and culture, we can generally say that statements about transcendence function as an extremely effective form of authority wielded by those who reference it to perform certain social functions that they deem desirable. These functions include providing certain individuals or groups social status, distinguishing insiders from outsiders, and granting to those who persuasively use it a relatively unquestionable form of power ("the sacred") that endorses their particular worldview.

It is important to state at the outset that one of the reasons why this sort of talk is so effective is not just because it can't be substantiated but also because its vagueness makes it into an incredibly pliable (and thus useful) tactic for justifying most every sort of political and social endeavor under the sun. Bruce Lincoln, a scholar of religion who is famous for his critiques of the methods used in religion's academic study, has noted that religious discourse is different from other forms of speech not because of its subject, but because of the way in which those who use it can reframe virtually anything as "sacred" (Lincoln 2003, 5–6).

Lincoln's functionalist treatment of religion (aptly named because it describes how religion works, or functions) helps us see that, contrary to popular belief, the distinguishing mark of religion is its ability to change the power dynamics between people by virtue of how they frame their perceptions of the world to one another. For instance, it is one thing if I say that I quit my job because my boss is unfair; it is an entirely different thing if I say I quit my job because God told me to. While both statements may be unverifiable for different reasons, the latter's reference to a transcendent force elevates that claim to a higher level of authority than the former if it is heard by an audience that is already sympathetic to religious ideas. As we will see, transcendence talk appeals to a very wide variety of people (both those who self-identify as religious and even those who don't) in great part because it performs myriad social functions, often in the span of just a few words.

Otto and Eliade: Manufacturers of "the sacred"

We can trace the academic practice of talking about transcendence as the central feature of religion to two noteworthy scholars, Rudolph Otto (1869–1937) and Mircea Eliade (1907–86). Although on their own they are each incredibly influential, considering Otto and Eliade together provides a more robust sense of why and how appeals to transcendence have been so popular.

Otto, a Christian theologian, is perhaps best known for his book, *The Idea of the Holy* (1923), a work that put him on the map as one of the twentieth century's most important thinkers on religion. Responding to critiques that studying religion is, essentially, the study of something make-believe, Otto's claim was that one can talk about a nonrational element of religion that is distinguishable from *irrationality* in the sense that religion doesn't disobey logic but simply stands outside of the boundaries of what logic is able to measure. Religion's essence, he maintained, is *sui generis*, meaning wholly unique, different, or "other"; because of this, Otto argued, religion defies not only the sort of analysis that we would normally use to discuss other social elements but also words themselves (Otto 1923, 7).

What Otto was thus attempting to describe is something that he (ironically) claimed was beyond rhetorical description. His strategy to logically study a nonlogical, unspeakable force was to examine the emotions that people experience when they claim to encounter such a thing, presuming that emotions were a sign of its reality (xxi). Otto described these emotions toward what he believed was this irreducible divine essence (which he called "the numinous") as absolute fascination, dependence, and, ultimately, mystery:

> The feeling of it may at times come sweeping like a gentle tide, pervading the mind with a tranquil mood of deepest worship. It may pass over into a more set and lasting attitude of the soul,

continuing, as it were, thrillingly vibrant and resonant, until at last it dies away.... It may burst in sudden eruption up from the depths of the soul with spasms and convulsions, or lead to the strangest excitements, to intoxicated frenzy, to transport, and to ecstasy. (12–13)

Although Otto's own identity as a Christian who was personally interested in interfaith cooperation will explain much of the thinking behind his model, his work had a much larger appeal. *The Idea of the Holy* was published just after the end of World War I, during what John W. Harvey, one of Otto's translators, describes as that "decade of disillusion" (x). Otto's ideas caught on quickly as his message of a common core underpinning the world's religions was met with great enthusiasm by a diverse readership happy to think of religion as a point of commonality that might heal the divisions amplified by the war (x–xi). As we will see, appeals to transcendence have long performed the work of rhetorically unifying diverse populations.

The notion that one can theorize and then objectively study a transcendent essence inspired another important figure of twentieth-century religion, Mircea Eliade. Eliade was so influenced by Otto that he mentioned the latter's book at the beginning of one of his own famous volumes, *The Sacred and the Profane* (1957). In many ways, Eliade's work can be read as a continuation of Otto's in the sense that it presumes a nonrational element to religion that is beyond the precise definition of the scholar.

Although in recent decades his popularity has waned, Eliade's contributions to the study of religion have been virtually unmatched, particularly when it comes to the practice of labeling social phenomena as instances of the manifestation of transcendence. Like Otto, Eliade assumed that a sacred essence permeates the world and manifests itself in various ways from time to time (manifestations that Eliade labeled "hierophanies"). "Religion" is the word that, to him, described the social institutions that have formed around these sacred emanations: "When the sacred manifests itself in any hierophany ... there is ... revelation of an absolute reality, opposed to the non-reality of the vast surrounding expanse. The manifestation of the sacred ontologically founds the world" (Eliade 1957, 21).

What Eliade was saying is nothing less than that the meaning behind everything around us is created by and from this sacred essence. In one of his other famous works, *Patterns in Comparative Religion*, Eliade catalogued the beliefs, rituals, and what he believed were the other salient characteristics of scores of different religious groups, presuming that the differences between each were just historical or cultural particularities that overlay an unchanging, sacred core: "Every manifestation of the sacred takes place in some historical situation.... The fact that a hierophany is always a historical event (that is to say, always occurs in some definite situation) does not lessen its universal quality" (Eliade 1996, 2–3). In this sense, Eliade's philosophical groundings remained strongly tied to Otto's claim that this presumed transcendent essence remains beyond human interrogation, for in his most consistent moments on the topic, Eliade described "the sacred" as something that people neither manufacture nor control—it simply appears and people respond, react, and build their cultures around it.[1]

Eliade's work has been used to much the same effect as Otto's was previously. Although his own politics have been the focus of much controversy, work produced by (and in the same vein as) Eliade has been used extensively since the mid- to late-twentieth century by interfaith and ecumenical groups, which are groups organized to create unity and find common ground between people of different religious affiliations. Such movements have capitalized on the notion of a common source underscoring all religions as a way to support religious unity, cooperation, and peace; they have also used this thinking to advocate for diverse political programs (such as campaigns to include discussions of non-Christian religions in American public school textbooks and questioning the degree to which Christian thought has been imposed on the public as the general standard of morality, as in issues such as abortion or gay rights).

While Otto's and Eliade's detractors have long argued that their models are not particularly academic (in the sense that they can't be proven—they are conjectured descriptions of conjectured things), our interest here remains how such speech can be made to mean any number of things depending on the speaker and his or her political inclinations. Even if one likes the outcome of such discourse (creating unity, peace, etc.), such situations echo Lincoln's earlier point that critically investigating religion is more about examining how it changes the power dynamics between people and groups than it is about the endorsement of a particular social or theological platform.

Scholars and the sacred

We've seen thus far that equating "transcendence" or "the sacred" with religion is not a particularly critical perspective, but it is certainly one that is quite political. By "political," I am referring to both the conscious and unconscious ways that certain perspectives reflect the attitudes of a specific group or provide it particular benefits. While Otto and Eliade generally presumed the objective reality of a sacred essence (which was among their own political contributions to the field of religion), their approach also paved the way for later scholars to use transcendence terms as if they are neutral adjectives when, in fact, they appear to be performing other important types of social work.

As evidence of this, consider Mary Pat Fisher's very successful *Living Religions* textbook series (now in its tenth edition), wherein she directly invokes Eliade when she writes that "[t]he sacred is the realm of extraordinary, apparently purposeful, but generally imperceptible forces. In the realm of the sacred lie [sic] the source of the universe and its values" (Fisher 2013, 10). She finishes that same chapter with a section that, while not drawing any specific conclusion about the relationship between religion and science per se, overall hints at the idea that the natural world has a mystical source (24ff). In this case, Fisher is positing the rather overt claim that there are invisible, transcendent forces that exist in the world and that those forces, known as "the sacred," comprise religion.

It is interesting that Fisher's forthright assertions of an unverifiable sacred essence figure so heavily in an academic textbook; keep in mind, however, that the success of a textbook is mostly gauged on whether it sells, and this is often determined to the degree that both professors and students like the content they find inside. It is also noteworthy that Fisher's online persona indicates that her primary credentials for textbook writing is her long-standing interfaith advocacy.[2] The fact that these are not normally the primary credentials of a scholar suggests, also, that her less critical approach is tolerated because of the sheer popularity of her claims.

However, most scholars hold the expectation that one must critically back one's claims instead of merely taking such things for granted. Because of this concern, many scholars will justify their references to transcendent forces by arguing that they are simply stating what religious people believe, and not necessarily evaluating the truth of the claim itself. Scholars of religion call this practice *epoche* (from the Greek, literally meaning "suspension of judgment").

On the surface, *epoche*—avoiding judgment of truth or falsehood—seems to be a rather reasonable way to proceed because it conveniently sets aside the controversies surrounding religion and allows scholars to simply describe what insiders say, do, or believe. But, as many critically oriented scholars have pointed out, there is a very thin line between describing what a group claims and actually including that claim in one's analysis. One of the most obvious ways that this line is contravened is when words implying transcendence are used without further explanation or qualification.

For instance, consider the following quotes from the written works of two prominent scholars of religion, Diana Eck and John Esposito. Eck and Esposito are both extremely well-known for their work on religious diversity, with Eck focusing on the Hindu tradition and American religious pluralism, more generally, and Esposito focusing on worldwide Islam. In the case of both scholars, the adjective "sacred" is used without explanation on numerous fronts to reference everything from physical places to books to music to symbols.

Note the following examples from Eck's well-known tome, *A New Religious America* (2002):

[Regarding the Hindu god, Shiva:] In Flint, Michigan, Shiva has his place in the center at the Kashi Vishvanatha Temple, named for Shiva as he appears in the sacred city of Benares in India. (85)

[Describing a Buddhist temple:] A few months earlier it had been dedicated and its sacred boundaries established during a week of festivities. (215)

[Describing the Hindu god, Ganesha:] It would be safe to say that all Hindus love Ganesha. They make a place for him in their home shrines and at the doorways of their temples, where he guards the thresholds into sacred space. (120)

In kind, here are excerpts from Esposito's book, *Islam: The Straight Path* (2004), wherein he also uses the adjective "sacred" in what seems to be the same sort of neutral, adjectival form:

> In contrast to Indian religious notions of cyclical history, rebirth, and personal perfection, the Judeo-Christian and Zoroastrian traditions affirmed a sacred history with a beginning and an end within which believers were to follow God's will and realize their eternal destiny in the next life. (8)
>
> Like all scriptures, Islamic sacred texts must be read within the social and political contexts in which they were revealed. (114)

While both Eck and Esposito avoid the appeals to sacred essences that Fisher performs, it is important to ask whether their description of certain things as "sacred" (or in the case of Esposito, we could add to the list "revealed") functions in much the same way. How does one know if the adjective "sacred" is simply a reference to what religious insiders consider sacred (and thus the scholar is simply mimicking the insiders' labels for the sake of description), or if the use of such an adjective is a sign that the author, too, takes for granted that the thing in question exudes some sort of transcendent quality?

A literal answer to this depends on the specific scholar and topic in question, and yet to some degree the fact that the scholar decided to use the insiders' terms to describe something that could otherwise be explained without that adjective (why call something "sacred history" when we could simply say "history"?) tells us as much about the politics of the scholar as it does the item under study itself. We can attribute much of this labeling tendency to the fact that, generally speaking, scholars tend to be progressive or left-leaning individuals for whom religion is often perceived as a fundamentally positive thing when it appears in its (also) progressive and left-leaning forms. In fact, plenty of scholars will advocate that religion's "real" or most "authentic" state occurs when religions celebrate diversity and pluralism, a position in line with most mainstream progressive visions. Conversely, most will talk about religion being "twisted" or "corrupted" or "counterfeit" when "bad" things (as the scholars define them) are performed by religious people.

Think of the considerable number of scholarly experts who are consulted by media outlets after some sort of violence is performed by a religious group or person. By and large, the role of this expert is to reassure the public that what happened does not reflect "mainstream (fill in the religion's name)," an assertion usually followed by the suggestion that the offenders have fundamentally misunderstood or otherwise twisted the "real" message of the religion, which would not condone violence. As Bruce Lincoln points out, however, an instance of religion is not defined by appeals to a transcendent force that is also progressive, peaceful, or unifying; the only marker for religion, he argues, is the transcendent appeal itself, whether or not we like the shape that it takes (Lincoln 2003, 16).

As we will see, scholars (and other public figures, for that matter) are willing to withhold the seal of transcendence from movements that they don't like—including everything from fundamentalist movements to terrorist groups—to make religion appear an institution that looks the way they wish it to be. Many scholars thus pay little heed to Lincoln's critique and, instead, throw their weight behind an image of religion that tends to be progressive and unifying in great part because it is necessarily vague.

The sacred is everywhere: Modern uses of the sacred concept

These same tensions over the concept of transcendence are also prominent in the ways that nonscholars speak about religion. Popular culture contains many explicit instances of "god-talk," a category that refers to notions of transcendence without using the overt language of organized religion and yet still clearly gets at the idea of a special or powerful sort of authority with whom humans relate. For instance, the group Alcoholics Anonymous (AA) famously references a Higher Power[3] (HP) in its directives to help people get sober, calling on the alcoholic to remember the power of the HP to "restore us to sanity" in its second of the famous twelve steps (Alcoholics Anonymous 2004, 25). In a similar self-help vein, Oprah Winfrey has frequently exhorted the public to remember that they are "sons and daughters of Creation" and should thus partake in the self-help advice she offers, since this elevated status makes them worth such personal improvement (Lofton 2011, 4).

AA and Winfrey may shy away from using the term "religion" or "God" (favoring, instead, "Higher Power" and "Creation") to describe their topic of interest if only because so-called organized religion has fallen out of favor with certain sectors of the public that often find it too limiting, dogmatic, or authoritarian. Its replacement with the ever popular term "spirituality" is, nevertheless, the same transcendent reference to religion in new clothing, for in each of these cases the point is to achieve or justify a particular goal by appealing to an authority beyond critique. Functionally speaking, then, AA and Winfrey reference a transcendent force to convince a group of people to conduct their lives in a different way, whether it is to stop drinking, to love themselves more, or to buy some of the media or literature that the two produce. This is a very powerful appeal because, as mentioned earlier, one feature of transcendence rhetoric is that it cannot be questioned; in other words, Oprah Winfrey cannot interview "Creation" to (1) prove that it exists or (2) see if it really does want people to have better self-esteem.

This rhetoric is also a central feature of the political realm. Americans may remember that the day after September 11, 2001, a group of politicians gathered on the Capitol steps to sing *God Bless America* and have done so periodically in commemoration of the attacks (Parkinson 2011). Why did they do this? It certainly wasn't because they were attempting to make a precise theological statement about a monotheistic deity; rather, the fact that this took place in public was intended to be a symbolic show of ultimate force against those who would aggress against the nation, as well as a show of unity to those affected by the attacks. In short, invoking the name of God functioned as both psychological warfare and a morale booster for the American public.

For a more extended example of the power of transcendence talk, consider the words of President Barack Obama at the 2015 National Prayer Breakfast when he mentioned ISIL, an acronym for a loosely affiliated group of radical Muslims associated with terrorist attacks. Obama's remarks to a religiously diverse crowd invoked the words "God," "faith," "belief," "good," and "evil" multiple times:

> [W]hat I want to touch on today is the degree to which we've seen professions of faith used both as an instrument of great good, but also twisted and misused in the name of evil.... We

see faith driving us to do right.... But we also see faith being twisted and distorted, used as a wedge—or, worse, sometimes used as a weapon.... We see ISIL, a brutal, vicious death cult that, in the name of religion, carries out unspeakable acts of barbarism.... And so, as people of faith, we are summoned to push back against those who try to distort our religion—any religion—for their own nihilistic ends. And here at home and around the world, we will constantly reaffirm that fundamental freedom—freedom of religion—the right to practice our faith how we choose, to change our faith if we choose, to practice no faith at all if we choose, and to do so free of persecution and fear and discrimination. (Obama 2015)

Perhaps it goes without saying that open displays of religiosity should be expected at an event with "prayer" in its title. However, it is important to recognize that the aforementioned concepts are not universally employed among all religions and, when they are, can often mean substantially different things. Rather than think of his statement as one that is characterized by a certain theological coherence, the fact that Obama didn't have to define these key terms for his otherwise religiously diverse audience indicates that something else was at work.

What this shows is that such terms, rather than functioning as particular theological checkboxes, were intentionally imprecise so that they would evoke some sort of positive group response. More specifically, this rhetorical act took place by juxtaposing concepts such as "freedom," "faith," and "great good" with other terms like "evil" and "vicious death cult[s]." Of course, ISIL members don't think of themselves as members of a vicious death cult, but this is part of the point: by reassuring presumably like-minded people that he, Obama, was like them ("good," "faithful," "believer") by virtue of their commitment to some common transcendent essence and by casting their mutual enemies as those who "twist," "distort," or "weapon[ize]" religion accordingly, Obama could both amplify his authority by appealing to a force beyond critique and unify a group of people who might otherwise be quite different. At the very least, the degree to which he used the word "our"—as if the audience and he shared some important commonality literally by virtue of being religious, no matter how or what that means—shows one important function of transcendence talk.

It should also have been fairly clear to most everyone in the room that Obama was using references to some sort of transcendent power to justify certain anti-terrorist political positions. Although invoking several potent symbols of harm at other points in the speech (including the Crusades, the Jim Crow era, etc.), he focused attention on the current political climate and the fight against Islamic extremism in the form of ISIL. When read from that angle, then, we can see how references to transcendence can do many things at once. In this case, they can simultaneously normalize the existence of the supernatural, identify an enemy, justify a political cause, amplify the seriousness of one's position, and unite a group of people under the banner of their own moral worth.

No matter the social realm we examine, then, it seems clear that multiple social effects are taking place when we talk about "the sacred" or a "higher power." Perhaps its most important role, as we have seen, is drawing boundary lines around people and their behaviors by creating a sense of unity that is made possible, in great part, because of the concept's utter vagueness. It is not hard to understand its allure, after all, since there is perhaps no more incredible power than convincing large numbers of diverse people to get behind a common idea, something that transcendence speech makes possible.

5

"Religion is a private matter"

Robyn Faith Walsh

During the 1960 presidential campaign, Democratic nominee John F. Kennedy faced the challenge of being the first Catholic candidate in a generation to run for the Oval Office and only the second Catholic to run for that office in the history of the country overall. With the possible exception of Abraham Lincoln, for whom there is little concrete evidence of religious affiliation, every US president to date—and since—had practiced some form of deism or Protestantism.[1] Kennedy represented a break with convention in a country that expected a president's religious beliefs to be a matter of public knowledge and debate. Consequently, the question Kennedy faced time and again from his political rivals as well as wary members of the electorate was, would a President Kennedy exercise his judgment independent of his church and its leaders?

On September 12, 1960, Kennedy attempted to allay public concern by giving a speech on what he termed "the religion issue" to a group of Protestant leaders at the Greater Houston Ministerial Association.[2] Frustrated that such a speech was necessary, he set aside what he considered "far more critical issues" (i.e., the threat of Communism, poverty, education) to explain that his religious beliefs should not be a factor in the election. Kennedy groused, "It is apparently necessary for me to state once again not what kind of church I believe in—for that should be important only to me—but what kind of America I believe in."[3] Reiterating his support for the separation of church and state as advocated in the First Amendment of the US Constitution, he continued, "I do not speak for my church on public matters, and the church does not speak for me." Finally, he cautioned that without religious liberty, "[t]oday I may be the victim, but tomorrow it may be you."

Kennedy's speech and the reasons he needed to deliver it illustrate many of the central issues surrounding the clichéd notion of religion as a private matter. Today, as then, the idea of religion as "private" is pervasive in the Western political and cultural imagination. This concept is often expressed by way of terms like "belief" or "personal experience" that emphasize interiority. Such language privileges hidden mental and emotional states. Further, the very use of the word "private" places religions apart from and unknowable to the outside world. This is why Kennedy felt authorized to claim that his belief "should be important only to me," that his church did not speak for him, and elsewhere in the speech, that his religious views were "his own private affair."

His strategic association between personal views and the oft-cited principle of the separation of church and state at various points in his speech allows him to imply that, though he might be a public servant, religious liberty under the First Amendment entails his exercising a separate, personal conscience, one that is subjective, private, and apart from his public responsibilities. As a general philosophy of liberal, democratic governance, Kennedy stands on solid ground. He clarifies that the Oath of Office necessarily prevents him from allowing his Catholic faith to influence his political decision-making. To drive this point home, he later quips: "there was no religious test at the Alamo." Nonetheless, his argument betrays an implicit conflict. As much as Kennedy would like to distinguish between his personal, inner life as a person of faith and his public, political life as a leader, the division is artificial.

There is no such thing as a "private" belief that can be held without some mediation by the social. Whether in terms of the practices, vocabulary, or symbolism associated with belief, religion is always embedded in a cultural context, framed by historical circumstances and informed by socially learned behaviors. Without a context for his Catholicism, Kennedy would have no language to deny the influence of Catholic leaders, to cite divisive issues for the Church such as birth control, to reference his conscience, or to advocate against religious persecution. The very fact Kennedy needed to address the matter demonstrates that religion is not some ineffable or transcendent thing that lives only in the mind of its practitioner. On the contrary, "religion" involves groups with shared practices and viewpoints. Further, it is inextricably tied to the larger framework of social living, even for those who deny that they are explicitly religious (see also Alexander and McCutcheon's chapter in this volume, "I'm spiritual but not religious").

Religion may be inherently social and, therefore, public, but it is common to describe it in private, subjective terms. While religious practice is often associated with organized institutions, practitioners of religion regularly express notions of personal morality, spirituality, and individualism when they communicate their beliefs. Such tendency is a result of Western philosophical ideas about the nature of "the self" and the self's relation to "religious experience." Drawing tight associations between religion and private mental and emotional states stems back as far as the Protestant Reformation in the early 1500s and the Enlightenment in the 1600s and 1700s. However, the more scholars rely on folk categories and self-descriptions to define what religion is and its role in modern life, the more imprecise we become about what we're talking about when we talk about religion. The result of such imprecisions is a tendency toward generalization (e.g., "baseball is my religion") or the kind of prejudice Kennedy warned against (e.g., "all Muslims are terrorists").

Understanding the roots of the concept of "private" religion reveals that religion is not some extraordinary personal concern. Instead, it is one of a number of rational positions that human beings take as they engage in the practice of ordinary social behaviors like group formation or identification with particular practices, organizations, and ideologies. Moreover, accepting that religion cannot be relegated to the false category of the "private" uncovers the ways it influences other aspects of daily life from one's relationship to the media, to the individual's participation in social institutions like marriage, war, and so on.

Clarifying this cliché

Before studying the history behind the idea of "private" religion, it is necessary to understand what a phrase like "religion is a personal matter" implies. Kennedy's Houston speech demonstrates the two tracks this cliché generally takes in popular culture.

The first track relates to contemporary ideas about citizenship. If the concept of religion as a social category appears odd, it might seem so because thinking about religion as integral to our social and political lives is not necessarily shared by everyone in the modern world. In a Euro-American, liberal-democratic context, citizens expect freedom of choice in terms of which religious institutions they choose to join. Further, there is little tolerance for religious organizations that meddle in how other religious groups, political bodies, secular institutions, or individuals conduct their business. Recall Kennedy's statement that he does not speak for his church on "public matters" nor does his church speak for him. Even if one considers religion fundamental to how society runs, it is often still assumed to be somehow conceptually apart from the broader fabric of politics, society, and culture.

The liberal democratic ideal of personal freedom, taken to its logical conclusion, sees the state as comprised of individual citizens with each pursuing their own self-interests. These include religious interests (see Arnal and McCutcheon 2013, 59ff). Some theorists have thus argued that religion is fashioned in contemporary consciousness as the "alter ego" of other social bodies like politics. While the word "religion" might evoke associations with institutions like synagogues, churches, or mosques, these associations are often secondary to the individual's private or personal pursuit of religious fulfillment. As one of the contributors to this volume, Russell McCutcheon—along with his colleague William Arnal—summarizes: "Religion ... is the space in which and by which any substantive collective goals (salvation, righteousness, judgment, condemnation, etc.) are individualized and made into a question of personal preference, commitment, or morality" (Arnal and McCutcheon 2013, 29).[4]

The second track for this cliché is that religion is the purview of every individual's subjective process of self-realization. "Private" in this case privileges the unique interiority of the individual vis-à-vis the symbols and practices of their religious tradition. Kennedy underscores this idea with his remark about the no religious test at the Alamo. Whether or not the men taking up arms there had a sufficient relationship to a particular religious tradition was a matter of their own, private concern—between them and their God. This understanding of religion is pervasive in modern culture, from daily devotionals to novels to comments on religion from public figures.[5] For example, when contemporary pop musician Rihanna recently remarked in a fashion magazine that "we are individuals with our own relationship to God," she was met with a groundswell of approving reaction from the general public (Sheeler 2014, 180).[6] Implicit in this construction is the notion that the religious commitments, desires, and self-understanding are ultimately inaccessible to the world outside the individual.

A caveat

You may have noticed several explicit references to "the West" or "Euro-America" thus far. It is important to understand that concepts of public versus private, religion, belief, individualism, and "the self" so common to this cliché are inventions of modernity and a "Western" cultural context. Before encountering the terminology of colonialists, words like "belief" were not used by practicing Buddhists in places like India and Sri Lanka where the emphasis lay on practices and disciplines.[7] Similarly, while the ancient Greeks and Romans distinguished in some measure between practices for the gods centered on the (private) household and acts performed (in public) with other citizens, these distinctions were not absolute, and nor were they expressed in the same individual, psychological terms we use today.[8] Even the concept of "religion" itself, at least as it is popularly understood in the modern West (that is, in terms of belief, experience, and privatization), likely would have been confusing to people from the past and might be still to many non-Western groups (see Arnal and McCutcheon 2013, esp. 29ff, as well as Asad 2003).

Still, it is dangerous to make sweeping assertions about any time period or region, and there may be examples that challenge any such generalization. As the anthropologist Talal Asad points out, while principally a phenomenon of "modern Euro-America," there are cases from "medieval Christendom and in the Islamic empires" that suggest the same shifts in philosophy and governance characteristic of the post-Reformation social order

(Asad 2003, 1–2). That said, modern Euro-American—and, even more to the point, Christian—discourse on the nature of religion remains the dominant influence on social and political history in the West. As such, that history will mark the parameters of this chapter.

The history behind the cliché

While there is no precise origin for the use of the "religion is a private matter" cliché, we can trace the trajectory of its development. Broadly speaking, the notion of religion as a matter of individual concern emerged alongside the rise of modern industrial society in the West. Advancing scientific and technological development coupled with urbanization and globalization decentralized the authority previously held by religious institutions. Scholars refer to this shift in the way people organized their local, day-to-day lives as the "secularization" of society.

The anthropologist Talal Asad along with the philosopher Charles Taylor describe secularization as a process by which people are classified as "citizens" rather than by other means, such as religious affiliation. In his *Formations of the Secular*, Asad explains: "[Secularization] is an enactment by which a *political medium* (representation of citizenship) redefines and transcends particular and differentiating practices of the self that are articulated through class, gender, and religion" (original emphasis; Asad 2013, 5). The secularization thesis reimagines the state as the framework within which citizens exercise their individual freedoms. Among these freedoms is freedom of religion.

Indeed, from the Protestant Reformation forward, religion was increasingly viewed as a matter of individual choice with churches no longer in a clear authoritarian lockstep with the state. Certain features from this period through the Enlightenment stand out as the foundations of our modern cliché.[9]

Reformation politics asserted significant challenges to established power hierarchies. A central consequence of those challenges was the validation of private judgment in the exercise of religious liberty. This validation challenged the rights of the state to dictate religious adherence to its citizens and questioned how the state drew the boundaries of religious liberty within established religious traditions (e.g., can an individual freely interpret scripture).[10] Technological innovations such as the printing press made popular participation in these debates more feasible and opened up new avenues for individuals to form and debate opinions. Religious studies scholar Elizabeth Pritchard describes this transition as the rise of the "modern public": "the image of religious dissent was transformed from brandishing a sword to picking up a pen ... religion's increased circulation in printed materials and the concomitant rise of the modern public [signaled] the transformation of religion's medium from bodies to speech and text" (Pritchard 2013, 19). Across Europe, people were able to assert new autonomy in their religious views and practices. In establishing the Act of Uniformity in 1559, for example, Queen Elizabeth I famously disclaimed that she did not wish to "peer into the windows of men's souls" and—in terms of public professions of faith—sought only the "occasional conformity" of once weekly attendance at Anglican services as a symbol of political loyalty.[11] Although it remained prescriptive, this measure signaled a recognition that religion was as much a concern of the interior life of the individual as it was a matter of outward performance.

A century later, John Locke, the so-called father of liberal democracy, advocated for broader religious toleration and further limitations on the government's role in religious matters.[12] In his *An Essay on Toleration* he avers: "For kneeling or sitting in the sacrament can in itself tend no more to the disturbance of the government or injury of my neighbor than sitting or standing at my own table" (Locke 1997, 138–9). What Locke termed elsewhere as "mere Religion" was still necessary for achieving "individual salvation."[13] However, so, too, was one's innate "liberty of conscience." For Locke, each individual should have the freedom to engage a public "diversity of opinions" about religion and then rely on one's own critical judgment to determine which religious institution to follow. This is what he considered "true" religion: religion based on "the inward perswasion of the Mind ... And such is the nature of the Understanding, that it cannot be compell'd to the belief of anything by outward force" (quoted in Pritchard 2013, 20). In other words, religious adherence was no longer solely a function of political dictate or familial inheritance, but a matter of personal self-reflection (quoted in Pritchard 2013, 22).

The Enlightenment marshaled ongoing debate over the legal authority of the Christian Church while simultaneously building on the Reformation ethos of individual liberty. The Declaration of Independence and the US Constitution were predicated on these philosophical positions—even if these documents applied such liberties only to free Caucasian men of European descent. Other writings of the so-called founding fathers reveal the depths of their individualist social theory. In his ongoing correspondence with John Adams, for example, Thomas Jefferson continually reiterated that, while religion should be openly debated, his personal religious views were by no means subject to public scrutiny. Rather, they were "known to my god and myself alone" (Cappon 1988, 506). Furthermore, Jefferson expressed eagerness for a time when advances in science and education would supersede dominating religious and political conservatism.

Elsewhere in the eighteenth and nineteenth centuries, discourse about personal conscience and secularization persisted in both popular and academic circles. The Romantic poet Samuel Taylor Coleridge, reflecting on what he termed "progression," declared that "Roads, canals, machinery, the press, the periodical and daily press, the might of public opinion" had effectively divided the British State from its religious roots (quoted in Kaiser 1999, 59). The sociologist Max Weber described secularization as the "rationalization and intellectualization" of the world, relegating religion purely to the sphere of the "personal" (Weber 2013, 155). Similarly, Weber's contemporary, the classicist and philosopher Friedrich Nietzsche argued that secularization and diversity had effectively displaced religion, rendering it on the margins of social regulation. In a published collection of aphorisms engaging the work of Descartes and Voltaire, Nietzsche explicitly labeled religion "a private affair" and a matter of "individual conscience and custom" (Nietzsche 1996, 171). By the twentieth century, these ways of talking about the private nature of religion were entrenched within the "modern public."

Moreover, throughout this renegotiation between religion and the state, religious institutions embraced the political philosophy of the individual and the personal. Once again, Asad helps describe this transition:

Several times before the Reformation, the boundary between the religious and the secular was redrawn, but always the formal authority of the Church remained preeminent. In later centuries, with the triumphant rise of modern science, modern production, and the modern state, the churches would also be clear about the need to distinguish the religious from the secular, shifting, as they did so, the weight of religion *more and more onto the moods and motivations of the individual believer*. Discipline (intellectual and social) would, in this period, gradually abandon religious space, letting "belief," "conscience," and "sensibility" take its place. (Asad 1993, 39, emphasis added)

Bolstered by a deeply rooted Cartesian tradition that bifurcated reality between body and mind ("I think, therefore I am"), material and spiritual, religion in modernity was no longer simply about following established doctrines or performing certain practices. It was also about what was unseen and interior (e.g., "believed"). Formal religious organizations remained, but just like politics, "religion" would come to be dominated by discourse on the private emotions, psychological states, and subjective judgments of the individual.

Still, in every case discussed previously, so-called private religion or private belief remains mediated by the social. Locke's concept of "true Religion" requires public discourse and debate for individuals to make judgments ("the inward perswasion of the Mind"). As Pritchard explains, "Locke is adamant that the highest duty for everyone (including the magistrate) is to attempt to persuade others as to what one regards as religious truth.... Locke envisions religion, including religious difference and dissent, to be precisely the sort of thing that ought to go public" (Pritchard 2013, 2). Similarly, despite Jefferson's protests that his religious beliefs were private, he discussed those beliefs publicly throughout his life. From the Declaration of Independence to the "Jefferson Bible," he openly engaged with deism and sought to convince others to abandon theologies he considered spurious.[14] As such, it is important to note that while rhetoric surrounding religion in the modern period increasingly focused on the private, this does not mean any actual phenomenon is being described. There is no point at which religion supernaturally transformed into a private matter. Instead, this description of religion developed over centuries in response to changing sociopolitical conditions, and the repetition of the idea through a variety of social networks further turned the claim that religion is a private matter into a cliché.

Religion as "private" in the study of religion

The field of religious studies has been complicit in the perpetuation of this cliché. The critical study of religion arose in Europe throughout the eighteenth and nineteenth centuries during the height of the Romanticist period. Naturally, scholars of that moment were steeped in the intellectual exchanges of the Enlightenment and Romanticist eras described earlier. Further, many of those scholars were religious themselves and inclined to use language born of their own religious practices. The biblical scholar and theologian Friedrich Schleiermacher, for instance, consistently described religion as *ein Privatgeschäft*—"a private affair" (see Schleiermacher 1996). In so doing, such thinkers perpetuated several facets of the cliché rather than critically analyzing religion's role in social activity. With some exceptions, it is only recently that experts in the field have recognized problems with these traditional approaches.

While religious studies scholars have begun to cast a critical eye on traditional methods, there remain intellectual inheritances that are difficult to jettison. One of the most enduring of these is the concept of private belief as central to religious activity.[15] Among eighteenth- and nineteenth-century Euro-American thinkers, "belief" was crucial to descriptions of religious activity. In one representative example, the nineteenth-century psychologist William James referred to religion as a "belief in an unseen order" (James 1985, 400).[16]

The definition of "belief" as the acceptance of a proposition in the absence of proof can be linked to philosophical circles dating back to the ancient Greeks. However, the definition of belief as an internal, personal commitment to intangible, religiously coded phenomena arises during the Inquisition and persists into the Reformation and beyond (see Schilbrack 2014, 59). Like "religion is a private matter," this latter iteration of "belief" is a product of the modern West.[17] Reference to an un-seeable, strong feeling continues to be pervasive in the academic study of religion to the present day. The twentieth-century anthropologist Clifford Geertz referred to contemporary understandings of religion as "attitude" (Geertz 1973). These scholars and the academic traditions they represent continue to hold great influence on the discipline.

"Belief" necessitates speculation about the unobservable and subjective. Unlike studies that consider discourses, social practices, or material evidence, academic work that prioritizes belief simply reiterates the descriptions of religious participants about their interior, mental states. The historian Bruce Lincoln offers a keen assessment of why "belief" is not a useful category for scholars of religion:

> Students of religion have no unmediated access to the beliefs of those they study, nor to any other aspects of their interiority. Rather, we come to know something of those beliefs only as they find external (always imperfect and sometimes quite distorted) expression in acts of discourse and practice. Regarding that of which one can have no direct knowledge, scholars cannot speak with any confidence and should—in their professional capacity, at least—perforce remain silent.... Belief almost never arises *de novo* in pristine interior reflection and experience, but generally follows exposure to the discourse of significant others. These include parents, above all, but also friends, family and clergy, who signal what they believe and what they (also the institutions and traditions to which they belong) believe ought to be believed. As these statements are received and metabolized by those to whom they are addressed, they are internalized as beliefs, but in this process, *discourse is both logically and chronologically prior to belief.* (emphasis added; Lincoln 2009, 111 n.15)

Lincoln's constructive recommendation is that rather than privilege "that of which one can have no direct knowledge," scholars should focus on what claims to belief signal in terms of social influences (e.g., language, politics, economics) and social networks (e.g., family, religious specialists). By examining *practices*, rather than claims about experience or private belief, scholars are better able to describe and analyze human activities, including actions and organized activities that are religious in nature. The religious studies scholar Stanley Stowers explains: "Practices (not individuals) carry 'understandings' that are expressed in doing and sayings" (Stowers 2008, 437). These doings and sayings, not belief or appeals to "private" sensibilities, should be our object of study.

Also contributing to the perpetuation of the "private matter" cliché is the unwillingness of some scholars to define religion *as* an object of study. This opposition has taken a number of forms, including those who persist in the notion that religion is ineffable (i.e., cannot be expressed in words) and, therefore, beyond description, and those who suggest that what we call "religion" is, in fact, nothing more than particular phenomena manifesting other aspects of social life—for example, politics (see also Arnal and McCutcheon 2013, 29ff). Perhaps one of the most influential scholars in the field today, Jonathan Z. Smith, has convincingly argued that the concept of religion should be defined and function as a second-order category for "the scholar's analytic purposes" (Smith 1982, xi). By generating such second-order categories, scholars are able to assess a variety of unique social practices in terms of their organization and how they are bundled with one another. One definition proposed by Stowers is that "[r]eligion consists of variously linked social practices (involving arrangements of entities at sites) that carry understandings involving the existence and activity of gods, ancestors, and various normally unseen beings, and that shade off into other anthropomorphic interpretations of the world" (Stowers 2008, 442). The benefit of a definition like this is that it is sufficiently flexible to be applied to both past and present, while avoiding culturally specific parochialisms like "private" or "belief." Increasingly, our task in religious studies is to reexamine our categories and how they function to inculcate certain understandings about the world. That is one of the objectives of this volume. Defining religion as students and scholars helps us avoid allowing popular discourse to be uncritically adopted when it should be part of our analyses.

Historicizing the present

When invoked, the "religion is a private matter" cliché accomplishes a great deal of rhetorical work. I have already discussed its history as a liberal democratic idea, and as an intra-Christian, Western discourse on the self. These connotations are inextricable from the cliché, even if one is not immediately aware of all of the conceptual and associative meanings it carries.

Use of this cliché also carries risk. Returning to Kennedy's exhortation on religious liberty ("Today I may be the victim, but tomorrow it may be you"), note that he is making a key observation about discourse that privileges the inaccessible, interior life of the individual. There is no objective measure by which one's private thoughts or commitments can be assessed. This makes such commitments both easy to fake and easy for someone on the "outside" to distort. Consider the political invectives against then Senator Barack Obama in the early 2000s that he was a "secret Muslim." Similar accusations persisted, in various incarnations, until the end of his presidency (Holmes 2016). These political attacks made no reference to what was known about Obama's religious practices (he had been a member of the Trinity United Church of Christ since the early 1990s; see "Obama Strongly Denounces Former Pastor" 2016). They had everything to do with the heterophobia of his opponents, utilizing a gross stereotype about Islam in the wake of September 11 to attempt to delegitimize his candidacy. Such a personal attack would not be possible without the pervasive notion in popular culture that there is such a thing as one's "private" religion.

This example also illustrates the importance of redescribing religion not in terms of private belief, but as a collection of "variously linked social *practices*" that focus on religious behaviors and their interface with other kinds of social activities (e.g., political, economic, etc.). Embedded in the political attacks about Obama's "secret" beliefs are a variety of "popular" and historically contextual discourses about religion in general, ethnicity, and religion in America at the turn of the twenty-first century. By allowing these kinds of discourses to be our data, rather than adopting our "folk" or clichéd conceptions, we gain a greater understanding of our social models and how to critically engage them.[18]

6

"Religions are mutually exclusive"

Steven W. Ramey

"Check one (and only one) religion." Such instructions are one way that we observe a manifestation of the cliché that religions are mutually exclusive. In many censuses, forms, and surveys that include religious identification, you can only identify with one religion because those who construct the instrument assume that identifying with a religion reflects an exclusive commitment. Those directions, and the ways the answers are recorded when someone does not follow the directions, directly influence the ways in which scholars and polling organizations report the number of Protestants in the United States or Buddhists in China. While this cliché is not always stated explicitly, it informs the assumptions that many people, including students, make about religion, that identifying with one religion excludes identification with or participation in another.

This idea intersects with the history of European knowledge about the wider world during the periods of exploration and colonization. Typically, Europeans assumed that everyone in the world had a religion and, more specifically, a singular religious identification, just like the Christians and Jews of Europe and their neighboring Muslims. The assumption of separate and exclusive religions contributed significantly to the development of the idea of the world religions. This assumption is also present in the questions of conversion and which practices a new convert to a religion must renounce and what they can maintain as part of their "culture." The assumption even has generated fear that people claiming to have converted did not truly reject their previous religious commitments and practices.

This cliché, though, is far from universal, as people in other parts of the world often have different conceptions. Many people in Japan, for example, participate across a lifetime in practices associated with both Buddhism and Shinto, seeing them as addressing different aspects of human existence. Some people understand all religions to be doing the same thing, allowing people to employ whatever practices or beliefs that they find beneficial. Within the context of South Asia, praying at the shrines and temples associated with different religions provides opportunities to access supernatural power or wisdom, without undermining a person's identification with one religion. For example, Qutb Ali Shah, whose followers in British India identified him as a Muslim Sufi, did not require his followers who identified as Hindu to convert to Islam. In fact, he incorporated deities and practices commonly seen as Hindu in his own activities (Gajwani 2000, 39–41), and Hindus and Christians who claimed a high social status often participated in each other's festivals as an expression of their higher status while excluding others who identified with the same religion from participating (Bayly 1989, 253, 289–90). Many people who identify as Chinese do not identify as a follower of any particular religion but follow practices that we commonly label Buddhist, Daoist, Confucian, and folk traditions. In fact, it is common for temples in Chinese communities to incorporate a range of figures that we commonly identify with different religions. Thus, the assumption that a religious identification excludes beliefs and practices associated with other religions is not a universal assumption but a construction that reflects the exclusivist nature of much of the theological reflections of proselytizing religions, specifically Christianity.

This cliché has a range of implications beyond the simple suggestion that anyone who participates in practices or accepts ideas associated with more than one religion is doing it wrong. The cliché informs legal decisions in some places, as a religious identification can have significant legal implications. It also appears in political rhetoric surrounding religion, both in the assertions that people of a particular religion should follow particular practices or hold particular policy positions and in assertions that label those who are identified with a particular religion as problematic, dangerous, or deserving of a diminished position in society, as such rhetoric assumes a commonality among those identified with that religion.

Therefore, this cliché has a prescriptive and predictive quality to it, empowering some to tell others how to act and assuming that someone will act in a particular way based on their religious identification. Rather than simply describing how people identify themselves, the cliché generates judgments that, if someone attends both a synagogue and a church, they are not being faithful to their religion. These assumptions can develop into a fear of corruption for some if they participate in something associated with another religion. The cliché also has a philosophical component, that the beliefs in one religion contradict another, making belief in both logically impossible.

Complicating this cliché does not mean that these alternate views about participating in practices associated with multiple religions or identifying with multiple religions are preferable. In any of these views, people make a variety of assumptions that construct the world and the concept of religion in particular ways. These different assumptions, then, promote different interests and forms of leadership in communities. Rather than looking for which way is the better way to view religions, this chapter will illustrate how this cliché (and the opposing views) is not simply describing things that exist in the world but creates and organizes that world in particular ways that support some and marginalize others, much as the survey data that others analyze reflects the constructions of the analysts rather than providing a neutral snapshot of the world as it is.

The unstated cliché

During the 2015 holiday season, the *Washington Post* ran a story that illustrates how pervasive this cliché is, pervasive to the point that it seldom is actually stated explicitly. In this human interest story, Rudri Patel, who identifies as Hindu, describes her choice to celebrate Christmas with her daughter, as well as celebrating Diwali, a festival associated with Hindu practices. Patel writes,

"Why do we celebrate both the Hindu holiday of *Diwali* and the Christian holiday of Christmas, which land on the calendar nearly at the same time?" (Patel 2015). In this rhetorical question, she acknowledges the common perception, the unspoken cliché in the United States, that someone who identifies with one religion should not be participating in another. In India, the question is unnecessary, as many people participate in Christmas activities or have an image of Jesus alongside deities commonly identified as Hindu within their home shrines. But in the United States, it is newsworthy and requires explanation.

The pervasiveness of the cliché is also apparent when someone fills out those forms or surveys that include a question about religious identification, whether it is a census form, a demographic survey, a college application, or a hospital admission form. While some forms now allow multiple responses to the question of race or ethnicity, including on the US Census since 2000, that option is not typically available on a religious identification question when a census includes that question. The form forces respondents to adhere to the cliché, even if they identify with more than one religion.

In relation to survey data, such singular identifications allow for a tidy table of affiliations. In one 2012 survey, 73 percent of the people in the United States identified as Christian, 19 percent reported no affiliation, and 6 percent identified with another religion (Pew Research Center 2012, 13). With almost 2 percent answering that they do not know, we have a standard 100 percent total between the different identifications. In surveys that also request details about specific practices and beliefs, it becomes clear that the singular identification that the survey requires does not reflect the limits of the respondent's practices, as people frequently incorporate practices and beliefs that are not officially a part of their religious community or identification. In some cases, people who identify with no religion participate in rituals associated with a religion, while some who identify with a religion do not see themselves as religious. This problem can become more pronounced when similar survey models have been applied to other cultures whose notion of religious identification does not necessarily adhere to this cliché (Johnson 2014).

When practices do not precisely match the identification, analysts perceive a need for explanation, much as the *Washington*

Post article's title suggested. For example, analysts have expended significant effort to explain the difference between the practices and the identification of those who had no religious affiliation in surveys (Bruinius 2015, Speckhardt 2015). Reflecting the pervasiveness of the cliché among English speakers, an English language magazine that is published by a Buddhist association in Japan dedicated a 2016 issue to the question, Can one practice two religions? Multiple articles in that issue answered the question in the affirmative and encouraged readers (primarily those outside Japan) to be open to a variety of practices from multiple religions, including the devotional and meditative practices that the Buddhist association promotes (*Dharma World* 2016). Assuming that someone who identifies with one religion and participates in multiple religions is doing religion "wrong" is a product of the cliché. For example, the British in India often assumed that people in India who followed practices that the British separated as Hindu and Muslim were ignorant about their own religion. Typically, any singular identification fails to convey the complexity of people's practices.

Legal structures also reinforce the assumption that a religious identification requires an exclusive commitment. In the adjudication in the US courts of the Free Exercise clause in the Bill of Rights (which bars the government from enacting legislation that prevents "the free exercise" of religion), petitions for an exception to a standard rule based on one's religion generally requires a singular identification that correlates to the requested action, under the rubric of a "sincerely held belief." In one 2015 case in which a college student argued for, and won, the right to join ROTC without shaving his hair or giving up his turban, the judge's decision asserted that he is "an adherent of the Sikh faith.... In accordance with his religion, plaintiff does not cut his beard or hair, and he tucks his unshorn hair under a turban.... Plaintiff maintains the sincere belief that if he cut his hair, shaved his beard, or abandoned his turban, he would be 'dishonoring and offending God'" (*Singh v. McHugh et al.* 2015, 3). The reference to "sincerely held belief" assumes this consistency, as the plaintiff (as in this case) describes the required practices or beliefs that go with identifying with the plaintiff's religion. The possibility of holding "sincerely held beliefs" that draw on multiple religions is not a practice generally recognized in American jurisprudence.

Interestingly, the legal structure in India, despite the fluidity of practice previously noted, holds to this singular identification in some contexts, including "personal laws" that deal primarily with family (marriage, adoption, divorce) and inheritance. Despite efforts to produce a uniform civil code, Indian personal laws vary between people identified as Hindu (which in this context includes Jains, Sikhs, and Buddhists) and people identified as Muslim and Christian. This legal distinction reflects the British practice when administering their colonies to avoid disrupting certain practices that the British associated with religion. Thus, the British maintained respect for differing religious practices associated with personal law, which has remained an issue in independent India. This procedure means that a singular identification is necessary legally, whatever practices a person follows, and the standard (though often contested) understanding of Hindu, Muslim, or Christian personal law limits a person's options.

The concept of conversion also assumes the cliché. The typical notion of conversion, often represented in Christianity by the story of Saul/Paul's conversion narrated in the Acts of the Apostles, involves a sudden and complete break from one religion to a distinct other religion, from Judaism to Christianity in this paradigmatic narrative. Such a notion of conversion requires the assumption that the two religions in question are not only clearly defined as different but also remain exclusive of each other. Conversion, thus, requires the rejection of the prior identification and the practices that went with it.

Sometimes, this aspect of the cliché is enshrined in conversion laws. In some parts of India over the past decade, laws have been passed that prohibit people from converting from Hinduism to Islam or Christianity without receiving approval. The rationale for the conversion laws was the protection of the poor and marginalized who (according to public discourse) were being induced to convert from Hinduism with financial and other material incentives. This construction assumes that conversion involves a break with a prior identification and practice that should be freely chosen. Beyond the issues of power in who can approve a conversion, the laws generated controversies, including questions about how different religions were grouped. Some of these laws implied that those who identified as Sikhs and Jains were counted as Hindu, despite their common assertion that they follow a separate religion. This controversy provides further evidence of the connection between conversion and the definition of exclusive religions, as well as the interest some groups place on their religion being recognized as distinct from others.

Scholarship, however, questions the starkness of this conversion paradigm, as often a shift in religious identification follows a more complicated process. Richard Eaton, for example, has studied the process of Islamicization in Bengal, a region on the eastern side of South Asia, now split between India and Bangladesh (1993). In his historical analysis, the development of an Islamic identification in the region was not a sudden shift by various individuals but involved a process in which people began to adopt new practices and then purified their practices by rejecting certain older practices, often at the behest of someone recognized as a religious authority. With continual shifts between adding new practices and ideas and purging others, an identifiable, new religious identification arose over time. Of course, the assumption remains in Eaton's account that the adoption of an Islamic identification reflects a change away from other practices and beliefs that are not recognized as Islamic. The notion of exclusive commitment to a single religion holds, even as the process is less distinct than often assumed.

The delineation of what constitutes each distinct religion also has been fraught with disputes. In what is known as the Rites Controversy in China, a debate arose among Roman Catholic missionaries over what practices were simply cultural (and thus permitted for converts to continue) and what practices were religious (and thus prohibited). Specifically, Matteo Ricci implemented greater acceptance of local practices, including the veneration of ancestors, in his effort to convert people in China to Christianity, arguing that these practices were cultural and not religious, but other missionaries argued that becoming Christian meant leaving behind these practices that they associated with another, erroneous religion. In both positions, we see clearly the assumption of exclusivity. The disagreement centered on the debate about what practices constituted religion, not whether conversion involves an exclusive commitment.

In addition to these legal and identifying practices, the common understanding of religion reinforces this cliché about exclusive commitment. As in the language of the US courts of "sincerely held beliefs," common understandings see religion as primarily about belief, and practices follow those beliefs. People generally assume that the various beliefs associated with a single religion should be consistent, forming even a single system of interrelated ideas. Practices then become the enactment and response to those systematic beliefs. Therefore, holding beliefs from multiple religions appears inconsistent (at least in common assumptions), and to participate in practices that enact contradictory beliefs, according to common understandings, would be either inconsistent or insincere.

The pervasive nature of this cliché is also evident in the structure of much of the academic world. Within both specialized research and textbooks for the classroom, this cliché often remains implicit. Even in textbooks describing a religion or the world religions, the language generally assumes a singular religious identification. A person is either a Protestant or a Catholic, a Pure Land Buddhist or a Tibetan Buddhist, so that even the subgroups of a religion are presented as exclusive of other subgroups in the same religion. Whenever people challenge that exclusivity by participating in practices associated with multiple religions, scholars often comment on that deviation because readers, and perhaps even some scholars, assume that the identification should match the practices.

Development of the cliché

How the assumption that religions are mutually exclusive became so enshrined culturally that it is seldom articulated requires some historical background. The typical view of religion comes from a predominantly European Christian context. In fact, the word "religion" is a European term that is not present in many cultures before European contact. While these non-European cultures had a variety of practices, texts, and ideas that came to be understood as religion, those particular elements were not necessarily grouped together as distinct from other cultural elements (Smith 1998; Nongbri 2013). As the term comes from European cultures, the aspects associated with religion are modeled on common images of Christianity, including the assumption that religions should involve an exclusive commitment to particular beliefs and practices. This assumption connects with the belief that only one religion can be correct and thus the concern among many who identify with Christianity to convert others to the one correct religion.

One aspect of the development of the idea of religion in the context of early modern Europe is an emphasis on the primacy of belief. The philosophical conflicts that we often identify in various schisms—from the early church councils that debated the nature of the divine and Jesus to the conflicts that arose in Europe that we call the Protestant Reformation—have significant implications for practices, but the issue of the correct belief is presented often as primary in those conflicts. In European thought, it is not possible for two different, conflicting propositions to be equally correct. Therefore, the emphasis on belief in the context of Europe makes the acceptance of the different ideas from more than one religion (and thus identifying with more than one) logically problematic, particularly considering the monotheistic background of most Europeans. Not only are the philosophical systems different (and thus often contradictory and not something that a person can hold simultaneously), but also many in the context of Europe emphasized the superiority of monotheistic conceptions that assume that the singular divine being excludes veneration of anything else. With the prominence of Judaism, Christianity, and Islam in the European construction of religion, it is not surprising that the mutually exclusive nature of monotheism common in each of those informed the construction of religion.

Notably, as Europeans explored and colonized other parts of the world, they often assumed that everyone had a religion and that their religion would have similar components to the presumed ideal form of religion, namely Christianity, making other religions inferior in most people's conceptions. One aspect of the European dominance during the era of expansion and colonialism was the development of the concept of world religions. The World Religions Paradigm refers to the delineation of distinct religions that each follow the paradigm of Christianity and remain exclusive of all others. The exact religions included in any world religion resource or text vary, in part based on the decisions of the authors and editors, but lists typically include at least five (Judaism, Christianity, Islam, Hinduism, and Buddhism) and often incorporate several others, such as indigenous religions, Daoism, Shinto, and Sikhism. The underlying assumption that each religion is distinct and identifiable enables the survey question asking respondents to select their (single) religion and the assumption that identifying with that religion precludes simultaneous acceptance of beliefs and practices associated with other religions.

Common lists of world religions have changed over time as people developed different notions of the broader world. Until the early nineteenth century, the more common listing included only four religions—Judaism, Christianity, Islam, and others (variously labeled pagan, heathen, etc.)—incorporating the lesser known practices and beliefs of areas outside Europe and its close neighbors into a single catch-all category (Masuzawa 2005, 46–7). Moving further back historically, some communities that identified as Christian followed a different construction, arguing that everyone is Christian and those practices and beliefs that most people now identify as different religions were simply heretical forms of Christianity (Nongbri 2013, 65–84). Between the disagreements over how to list religions now and these historical shifts, no list of world religions reflects a simple description of a reality that exists, yet the lists themselves assume a distinctiveness of each religion that generally reinforces the assumption of exclusivity.

While the dominance of the cliché in Europe and the Americas (with the significant settlement of Christians from Europe) fits this background, the power of the cliché to influence the legal structures in a place like India, where these ideas were not automatic, provides a further puzzle. Research on colonial India has suggested that the stark boundaries dividing what the British labeled Hinduism and Islam were constructions of the British. Prior to the colonial period, the practices and identifications were more fluid as some people engaged in practices that we typically associate with distinct religions and maintained ambiguous identifications. In the context of nineteenth-century India, British colonial officials applied strict definitions (that they developed in conversation with some indigenous leaders) to distinguish Hindu and Muslim identifications. This led to some difficulties, as the census takers had to determine the correct identification for respondents for whom such questions were strange. Identifications have become more rigid in India, in part as an outgrowth of the census process and other aspects of the colonial administration of India, leading to the Partition of British India in 1947 between Muslim and Hindu majority areas (roughly) based on that census data. Nevertheless, many in India continue to participate in practices commonly associated with multiple religions, and many people see no problem with both a singular identification and the range of practices that the individual considers significant for them.

The power of the cliché

One trait of what people sometimes call New Age religion is the adoption of practices associated with different religious traditions, which becomes a point of critique for some people opposed to New Age practices. A similar issue arises in the language of "spiritual but not religious," which rejects institutional forms of practice for an individualized selection of practices. Academic responses to such processes have sometimes included problematic criticism. For example, when an interviewee (Sheila) described her idiosyncratic practices to researchers, as detailed in the *Habits of the Heart* volume, the authors bemoaned her construction, labeling it "Sheilaism" because it was unique to her and had no institutional basis (Bellah et al. 1985, 221). For some, idiosyncratic combinations illustrate the problem of the breakdown of religious discipline and institutions, as they preferred an idealized construction of each religion. However, for others, these examples have suggested that the boundaries that many have constructed to separate religions are quite porous. The assumption that following a religion properly, as the tradition and institution constructs it, is preferable remains in some academic work. This assumption, then, empowers the institutions and their recognized leaders to determine what is appropriate practice.

A more recent academic discussion of these instances of individual selection of disparate elements is the metaphor of a spiritual marketplace in which individual consumers select the practices and ideas that are relevant to them (and ignore those that are not) without concern for the boundaries dividing religions. This discussion, while at times bemoaning the loss of tradition and discipline, enshrines a particular image of religion as involving community and traditions while also reinforcing the contemporary assumptions of individual freedom. However, even though the range of practices available today is greater in many parts of the world than they were two centuries ago, many people at that time also had choices, participating more enthusiastically in some practices than others and including practices that religious institutions identified as outside the boundaries. For example, in the British colonies that became the United States, those identified as Christian incorporated astrology and similar practices despite the common Puritan teachings that such practices were not acceptable for people who identified as Christians (Hall 1989).

Such examples, whether contemporary or historical, also reveal some of the power dynamics involved, as religious leaders and institutions—particularly in the context of Europe and the Americas—use the assumptions that the cliché represents to maintain their authority and control. The notion that a person should only follow one religion gives power to the prohibitions of community leaders who assert the specialized knowledge, and thus power, to define what practices were a part of their religion and what practices they identified with another religion or as opposed to religion. For example, a church leader who declares that yoga is anathema to Christianity asserts authority over church members that also reinforces the leader's broader authority to declare certain practices as appropriate to be included in this identification. The restriction of religious identification to a single, distinct religion becomes a useful, even powerful, tool in modern society, as the leadership in religious communities and even the nation-state use this cliché to order society and increase their ability to control those in their community. Thus, the consequences of this cliché extend well beyond the simplification of census and survey data.

As we have seen already in discussions of the personal laws in India and free exercise cases in the United States, legal systems often assume exclusive religious identifications, giving the government power to oversee religion. Beyond general government power to regulate these activities, those who become the interpreters of religion, of what is proper for a person identifying with a particular religion, have considerable power. The All India Muslim Personal Law Board, for example, determines the applicable laws for those who identify as Muslim, and expert witnesses in US court cases can have considerable influence in determining what counts as proper religious practice. During the colonial period in India, those individuals who were trained in Sanskrit and the various Sanskrit texts, both priests and scholars, held a significant position interpreting Hindu practices and requirements for the British. If someone identifies with multiple traditions, they create fissures in this system of legal recognition and present challenges to both governments and these interpreters of religions. Thus, the assumption of a singular, exclusive commitment establishes an ordered world in which the practices that the government recognizes as protected or acceptable can be clearly defined. This concern functions in the same way for census takers and polling processes. The standardized identifications prevent more complicated issues from arising and enable a more efficient management of the population for governmental powers.

This power and ordering of the world is particularly visible in the contemporary popular discourse about Islam, which assumes that an identification as a Muslim represents a complete commitment to the ideas associated with Islam. Certainly, both those who identify as Muslim and those as non-Muslim present many conceptions of the ideas that they associate with Islam. For some, it is a religion of peace that requires hospitality and respect for all, while some identify Islam with violence against non-Muslims. Whichever position a person presents, implicit in that assumption is that everyone who identifies as Muslim adheres or should adhere to that position. Thus, individuals who participate in practices associated with other religions, like Qutb Ali Shah, or who enact the opposite view of Islam, are assumed to be bad Muslims. While the cliché generates a simple world where everyone has one identification and their behavior is predictable based on that identification, human activity is more complex. The desires of the nation-state to have definite, exclusive identifications also inform particular policy proposals. In the context of the civil war in Syria and the rise of the Islamic State in 2015, some politicians in various countries have proposed to limit the acceptance of Syrian refugees to those who are Christian, assuming that the religious identification predicts behavior and that such a religious identification is an easily verifiable aspect of a person's life. Identifying people by religion, though, is not a simple task, especially when policies construct different treatment based on that identification.

This cliché has faced critique but remains powerful in constructing an ordered world that empowers some to define appropriate practice for others. Nineteenth-century British officials in India sometimes asserted that the people of India too often did not know their own religion and, in at least one case, prohibited Christians from participating in a Hindu festival because the officials assumed that Christians would only participate under duress, when, in contrast, participation seems to have confirmed a high social status (Bayly 1989, 289–90). More recently, some scholars have celebrated such participation across presumed boundaries, seeing in such flexibility the hope for the reduction of conflicts that many connect to the differences separating communities (such as Hindus and Muslims in India). Yet, others in India have increasingly emphasized difference and strict boundaries, such as non-Hindu community leaders discouraging some from participating in public yoga sessions, with only limited success (Jain 2016). These different approaches illustrate how both the cliché and alternates often become a means of promoting particular interests and ideological positions. Recognizing the power and assumptions behind this cliché does not mean that the alternative visions of practices and identification is superior but highlights one way that common assumptions about religion are not as universal and unquestioned as contemporary discourse suggests.

7

"I'm spiritual but not religious"

Andie R. Alexander and Russell T. McCutcheon

It's relatively easy these days to hear someone say, "I'm spiritual but not religious"—sometimes abbreviated as SBNR. But in our experience it's not the sort of thing people just go around saying, unprompted; for, much like declaring your love of chocolate, where you're originally from, or your college major, it's usually stated as an answer to a question, asked and answered in a specific situation— such as the time that one of us was shopping for furniture in a new city, having just moved there. Learning that we were new to town, the salesperson asked, "Have you found a church-home yet?" There's a variety of answers, to be sure, from "Yes I have" or "No, but can you suggest one?" to "I don't believe in God" or maybe even "Why are you asking me that?" Among the imaginable answers to this query would be, "No; I'm spiritual but not religious."

This chapter is curious to figure out what might be going on in that moment, during that exchange. And, given our experience studying human behavior, our hunch is that the social actors involved don't necessarily know all that might be involved in these seemingly simple questions and answers.

So, right off the bat, the first thing to be noted when we consider this now common phrasing is that saying "I'm spiritual but not religious" (much like saying or writing anything—but more on this later) is the tip of a social moment, evidence of a specific situation in which a speaker is interacting with someone—someone with expectations, hence the question. (No doubt that store clerk had a recommendation ready at hand, if that's where the conversation had gone.) Now, of course, this is not something you're probably thinking to yourself when you say this to someone; that is, when someone answers, "I'm spiritual but not religious," our guess is that such speakers likely think that they're making a claim about some interior state or awareness that they possess or have experienced—call it spirituality, perhaps—that, again they likely presume, somehow operates outside of, or prior to, the restrictions of institutional settings—something they'd likely call either "church" or "religion." So when that salesperson inquires if you've "found a church-home"—implying an institution with membership and regular attendance, as well as sets of rituals and periodic ceremonies, potluck suppers, and church basement socials, etc.—this reply makes a claim that all of these institutional trappings are somehow nonessential; instead, or so this reply seems to say, a claim is being made that there is something that predates them all, operates outside them all, some interior disposition unique to certain people, maybe some insight or affectation that, whether complementary with "going to church" (or mosque, synagogue, or temple, to be sure), certainly doesn't require it. (In fact, some might even claim that the institution limits or stifles it.) It's an answer that, to the one making the claim, therefore seems to involve (either explicitly or implicitly) a bit of an arm wrestling match, for it takes a widely accepted notion of religion and somehow one-ups it, as if one can have all of the benefits of some sort of deep interconnection with the universe (or however we might broadly define this word religion) without having to get dressed up each week.

But regardless what those who say (or identify as) SBNR might be thinking (or how the store clerk might have heard it, if that's what we had answered), to the scholar of religion there are some interesting things going on here that should cause us to pause for a moment and not simply accept the view that, while this thing we call religion is boringly lodged within repetitive rituals and traditions, this alternative thing that some call spirituality is somehow in step with each of our truest, deepest, and most authentic and unique selves. For it doesn't take long to realize that the way this term spirituality is now being used—as if it names some pre-social and thus institution-free insight or feeling (dare we call it spirit?) that someone just has or somehow senses—is itself part of a tradition and, yes, like all institutions, has a history. It's therefore no little irony—and this is *precisely* what makes this so interesting to look at in a new way—that from *within* tradition and *within* history people are making claims that are thought to be free of tradition and untainted by history.

Case in point: think back to the opening of this chapter, when we imagined someone replying, "I'm spiritual but not religious." Not only should we take seriously the social moment of the exchange (i.e., as far as we know people don't go around spontaneously saying such things; this is part of a conversation) but also, to press this point even further, we must keep in mind that this is language and none of us made up our own language (if we had then we certainly wouldn't be talking to anyone else). Instead, we were all *taught* a language—we memorized vocabulary and spelling, along with all of the rules of its grammar and syntax (who among us doesn't know "i before e except after c"?)—all of which predated us, considerably. Members of a previous generation (or even our older siblings) leaned in close and rubbed our little tummies and whispered things in our ears; they told us that "the farmer drives a tractor" while flipping through the pages of a picture book, singing the ABCs song, and they eagerly awaited our first words—words spoken in whatever language into which we happen to have been born. It's therefore no coincidence that most who read this text are native English speakers. So the irony grows even deeper, even richer, making it all the more fascinating, when we consider that a speaker who says SBNR seems to think they're making a tradition-free, authentic claim about some interior dimension that they possess but they do so in the most tradition-bound of settings: language. For if you stop and think about reading this very text, and all of the rules the writer and reader must share and follow for it to seem to make sense to us—despite having never met each other and, for all you know, living thousands of miles apart and being members of drastically different generations—well, it can lead one to find very curious anyone who thinks that they can somehow opt out of institutions and traditions. (In fact, don't institutions have an institutionalized way to leave them? This suggests that we never really can leave institutions behind, for in opting out, in the proper way, we further mire ourselves within them. Another irony . . .)

So, rather than assuming that only one side of the SBNR divide is somehow authentic and pure, it may make more sense to conclude that what we may have on our hands, whenever we hear someone say SBNR, is a glimpse into a social moment when members of one tradition, embedded within institutions with which they're familiar, contest others while seeking to authorize themselves. But to reach that conclusion—to develop a social theory of SBNR discourses— we need to back up a bit and reconsider the very model of meaning-making that many of us walk around with in our daily lives; for asserting that a pre-social moment of pure spirituality exists is something that we can claim *only* if we assume that language is a neutral medium by means of which we *express* (and that's a key word to which we're going to return) things that are already somewhere inside our heads, that we call meanings. But if that's not the way meaning-making actually works (and the fact that we commonly call it meaning-making is already a clue to rethinking these clichés, for maybe our labor is involved more than we know, making us hardly passive observers in the process), then maybe there's a way to hear "I'm spiritual but not religious" differently and see this claim as part of the mundane, day-to-day arm wrestling match that is social and historical life.

Making meaning

Knowing that's where we're going in this chapter, let's back up and start over again, but this time in order to think in a more focused manner just about how meaning works—and so we don't mean anything terribly sophisticated, just everyday meanings—such as reading signs downtown or reading your friend's body language. Or maybe the act of reading, as you're doing now, these inked and printed markings that we call letters, punctuation, and words. Or talking and listening, in the most mundane of ways—riding a bus we hear a bell ring and know that it *means* the bus is making a stop.

But do you remember the first time you rode a public transit bus? Did you instinctively know what the ding meant? Our guess is that you didn't; as with language, you needed to be trained by others who came before you, those who knew the ropes, as it were. So, as previously stated, the difference between how we commonly think about this process and how this process of meaning-making might in fact work may help us unpack what's going on when someone distinguishes (and then ranks—a crucial element of the distinction!) spirituality from religion.

So let's reconsider the work involved in everyday conversations. Oftentimes we have varying types of conversations, all depending on the audience with whom we are speaking. That is, the way in which one would greet an old friend is likely quite different from how that same person would greet a professor or dentist. There would likely be a level of formality employed when conversing with either of the latter—maybe we'd signal this by means of a title—that was not there when meeting the longtime friend. That is to say that our ways of communicating are dependent on the specific situations and the degree of familiarity with a particular audience or conversation partner. So, contrary to our commonsense model, one that assumes meanings are first on the inside and are then secondarily projected outward into the public domain (a key aspect of SBNR claims), it may instead be that language is not some neutral medium that merely carries our interior meanings; instead, the very things we call meanings might be the product of the situation itself—making meaning a far more social thing than we had at first imagined.

Thinking ahead, if the situation (e.g., meeting your sibling at the mall versus meeting the mayor in town hall) dictates how we talk, then what might the implications be for those SBNR claims?

This situatedness is probably evident to those studying a foreign language. At the undergraduate level, many of us are required to take several semesters of a foreign language as part the core curriculum of our degree. As an undergraduate at the University of Alabama, one of us studied Italian to fulfill those requirements. Throughout the semesters of language training, we quickly learned that translation from Italian to English and from English to Italian was not, as we had at first assumed, a one-to-one correspondence, as if merely converting inches to millimeters or kilos to pounds. That is, rarely is there a verbatim translation of one language into another—the words work within different structures (i.e., the rules of different languages) and so are not necessarily ordered or structured in the same way and the grammar and syntax likely vary, sometimes closely related and sometimes drastically different. When these sentences, words, phrases, and clauses don't line up exactly, the translators must do some artful interpretation of their own so as to move the meaning they derive from one sentence to another, thereby moving from one communication system to another. And to anyone who immerses themselves in this task, it soon becomes apparent that different languages (especially languages that do not share a common ancestor), each with different rules, make different meanings possible; so what soon becomes apparent is that the widespread model which assumes a common, static, inner meaning that is merely *expressed* (there's that word again), in one code there and another here, quickly fails. Instead, when matched up against each other, the systems are separated by gaps, leaving considerable room for ambiguity and difference when they are compared (as a translator might)—like the time one of us had a book translated into modern Greek and were told that there was no available word in Greek to convey all that the technical term "discourse" (an English translation of a French original) has come to mean for current scholars, for it means so much more than just talking.

Varying interpretations of sentences and the many different word choices are why many language teachers warn students against using Google Translate to aid in their homework assignments. For despite how grammatically accurate the sentence translated in this manner may seem, a particular translation may not fit the situation and therefore would be graded by the professor as incorrect. For instance, consider this example of an English to Italian translation after typing this sentence into the Google Translate box:

We are going to the square for ice cream this afternoon.

Google provides us with the following Italian translation:

Stiamo andando al quadrato per gelato questo pomeriggio.

Following our commonsense model of language and meaning (which assumes a universal meaning exists on the inside of our heads and which is then expressed), this translation is a word-for-word match and, technically, correct by Italian grammatical standards; however, if you were to use this sentence in conversation, you would likely get some funny looks from the people with whom you're speaking. For while the sentence does make rudimentary sense, some of the words used would likely give away the speaker as an outsider or non-native, because the language and structure aren't quite right. For example, in Italian conversation, as we were taught in class, gerunds (words that look like verbs but are not) are often dropped and are replaced with the present active voice ("We go"). So in casual Italian conversation, one would not necessarily say *Stiamo andando* ("We are going"); instead, one would more than likely say *Andiamo* ("We go"). Furthermore, "the square" mentioned in the English sentence (e.g., a town square) can, indeed, translate to *al quadrato* but would more accurately translate to *alla piazza* (also, "the square"), referring to the town center where one would likely find a few ice cream shops, or *gelaterie*. What's more, the end of this example sentence, *questo pomeriggio*, is a literal translation of "this afternoon," but in Italian, the more common conversational form would literally translate to "in the afternoon" or *nel pomeriggio*. So while this Google translation certainly isn't *wrong*, if used, the sentence would show a lack of fluency and constitute evidence that you failed to possess the understanding that a native speaker or well-trained student might have.

So instead of

Stiamo andando al quadrato per gelato questo pomeriggio.

the more appropriate version of this sentence would be:

Andiamo alla piazza per gelato nel pomeriggio.

While the Google translation may be grammatically accurate, that version is not necessarily appropriate for certain situations (such as speaking to an actual Italian with whom you would like to go for ice cream—though, what we call ice cream and what they call gelato are hardly the same thing, which again makes our point!). From this we can see how quite a bit of work, even art, goes into moving from one language to another—students in language classes have surely experienced this frustration on more than one occasion—and that translations, more often than not, require a great deal of interpretation to create the right meaning for any given circumstance.

Moral of the story?

Translation is best not thought of as a mere conversion or a search for the matching words, but rather a creative move between different code systems that each make different meanings possible. Skilled translators, then, are people who are prepared to make leaps more creative than just knowing that 0.621371 kilometers precisely equals a mile, and thus they're bold enough to let go of some things that are inexpressible in one language (e.g., we have ice cream, not gelato) and to hold on to, in some newly reshaped form, yet others. For, like that old saying goes, there is indeed something lost in the translation—not the meaning, but rather the ability to frame, even to make, certain meanings.

Situated meaning

Considering the level of (often unrecognized) work that goes into even just everyday conversation—that is, speakers engaging with one another in particular ways depending on their audience and situation—we can see how very simple exchanges are an excellent place to revise the way in which we think about meaning (and thus the common model, so essential to SBNR claims, that assumes significance is internal and is only secondarily expressed). Since we're already knee-deep in the example of Italian conversation, let's consider a standard Italian greeting, one that many of you are likely familiar with: Ciao. If asked what *ciao* meant, anyone with a rudimentary knowledge of Italian would likely tell you that it means "hello," but, then again, they might also tell you that it means the exact opposite as well: "goodbye." (Question: how does one know when it means which?) But some might tell you that *ciao* is an informal greeting, much like "Hey, how's it going!" or "What's up?"—a greeting that requires the intended audience only to repeat the same word back as the response: "Ciao!" (Come to think of it, this is not all that different from answering "How's it going?" whenever someone passes you and says "How's it going?") So, depending on the situation—that is, whether one is arriving, leaving, or just passing a friend (as opposed to your boss) on the sidewalk—*ciao* can have all sorts of meanings and can be translated, or interpreted, differently for each.

While this may seem at face value to be all too obvious, this simple social exchange (a greeting) can help us reconsider the level of work that goes into everyday conversation—that is, it's not a matter of actors *expressing* meanings that are already in their heads but making up meanings by examining the situation in which they're embedded. (Isn't that precisely how we figure out if "ciao" means hello or goodbye?) Of course "work," in this instance, does not necessarily mean labor-intensive, for native or fluent speakers converse easily because they are well trained—they're benefiting from work invested over the course of their entire lives or years of study. (Such as you reading these very words.) So, for one to adequately translate this social exchange of an informal *ciao*, one must determine the fitting meaning (hello, goodbye, etc.) for a given situation, since it would look a bit strange if a movie subtitle translated *ciao* as "hello" if the speaker said it as they were exiting the movie scene, no? So despite the simplicity of *ciao*, definitionally speaking, it nicely illustrates an important point: the situatedness of the conversation and those doing the speaking determine which meaning we should or should not use and understand.

Or, for another example, consider a common phrase that we have at the University of Alabama, where one of us works and the other did an undergraduate degree: *Roll Tide*. While to many people this phrase would likely be directly associated with the *Crimson Tide* (i.e., the university's football team), to a native Alabamian and, more especially, to anyone affiliated with the University of Alabama (such as a student or football fan), the phrase *Roll Tide* can have any number of meanings. Perhaps you saw ESPN's "Roll Tide" commercial that aired back in 2010. In this short commercial, we see many instances of people saying "Roll Tide" to one another yet the intended meaning varies with each setting. Aside from meaning "go team," this phrase is also used as a passing greeting, saying thank you, or concluding a wedding speech and even a preacher ending his eulogy, among others portrayed in that commercial. Much like the Italian *ciao*, the meaning of *Roll Tide* is necessarily dependent on the social situation and can be used in any number of ways—ways that would unlikely translate well to anyone unfamiliar with this interaction. For an outsider, as with outsiders to any language, the phrase would be odd if not unintelligible. Yet when speaking to members of an in-group—that is, people who either interact in this way or are at least familiar with this social interaction—the phrase *Roll Tide* can be a way to reinforce a particular identity that the speakers may both adopt and share; it amounts to a form of social grooming—"I identify with the University of Alabama, do you?" it asks, awaiting the "Roll Tide" reply if the answer is yes. (Here's another exchange where the same thing is said by both parties.) However, if one were to say *Roll Tide* to a student or person affiliated with Auburn University—Alabama's rival in-state school—the recipient of that "Roll Tide" would likely retort (in jest or, perhaps, in anger) with Auburn's parallel phrase, "War Eagle," and so, rather than establishing a connection with that person, the phrase "Roll Tide" would function to create and then mark a divide. And while it's important to recognize that neither of these phrases really *mean* anything—they are just words associated with the schools' sports teams and do not necessarily signify this or that—a particular meaning ("We're allies!" or "We're antagonists!") can be created depending on the situation and social actors involved. For it can be a congratulatory statement, a way to bond with others, or a way to establish difference, but this is only evident when we, the users of language, understand and analyze meaning based on the situated, and observable, social interaction. Put differently, much like translating that sentence from English to Italian, we must consider the setting, the speakers who are interacting, and the structure (and thus limits) of the language in which they're working, for the meaning produced can vary with each.

These examples, though straightforward in many ways, hopefully begin to highlight the complexity of meaning—that is, thinking back to the start of this chapter, to begin to make the point that meaning might not somehow preexist language, and thus might not be floating privately in the speaker's mind, disengaged from the world until it is spoken or written; for it is just as much rooted in a social and historical context as are all conversations or all interactions with a text. In fact, since we were all taught language by others, who came before us, you could even go so far as to say that talking to yourself (or thinking a thought) is still very much part of a social exchange and thus a conversation—a conversation with all who came before you and who developed the language that you now speak (and, yes, tweak as well).

So when we explore the largely unnoticed—or perhaps ignored or, better put, just unrecognized, since we're each just so used to doing what we do (and it is a *doing!*)—work that helps establish the apparent self-evidency of those sounds that we make, such as "Ciao" or "Roll Tide," then we can begin to see the thing that we at first take to be interior, that is meaning, in a whole new light: as a social process of meaning-making, a type of shared and always public labor that, depending how it is done, has practical effect, such as distinguishing a this from that, or an us from a them—such as that Auburn fan not looking too kindly on the "Roll Tide" greeting.

Not Taking Meaning for Granted

So now, thinking back to where we started this chapter, maybe you can see why we took that detour to rethink how meaning works. Let's start *not* with the lone individual thinking (and thereby owning) their solitary thoughts and then pushing them outward (literally, what "express" has traditionally meant) into the world, where they're prone to be misinterpreted by those who hear them but who don't properly understand the speaker's intentions ("That's not what I meant"). Instead, if we reconceive all speakers and writers as always involved in an ongoing, public conversation with others, with all parties being involved in the meaning-making, since they all work with an already-made and necessarily shared script and set of rules—a script and rules that make certain things possible to think and say and other things impossible (after all, you can't play ping pong on a tennis court no matter how similar the games appear)— then what do we make of someone who comes along and says: "I'm spiritual but not religious"? For, as already suggested, this claim (at least as understood by some who make it) seems to signify that there exists something pre-social, something this person (and not that—the one who simply identifies as being religious, we guess) possesses or experiences that is more deeply significant because it is outside of (i.e., preexisting) all institutional constraints. While our commonsense way of understanding ourselves might suggest that such a claim is sensible—lots of people seem to think it sensible to say it—the excursion we just took into an alternative way of thinking about meaning now suggests that such assumptions are rather problematic, inasmuch as they seem to take the social work and thus institution-specific setting of all meaning-making as invisible, as if it wasn't even there. And, failing to see all of the social actors and social work that necessarily came before them, they assume that they came up with it all on their own and that they stand apart, as distinct and individual, from the many others who make it possible for each of us to make sounds and markings that our peers take to be meaningful. (For instance, are we making the meaning as we type this very line, or are you making the meaning as you read it?) What's more, there are many ways of understanding how to be authentically SBNR, which further demonstrates the continued social contest and arm wrestling involved in maintaining (because it too requires work) some notion of spirituality as distinct and private, preexisting the social and the institutional.

And of all the things that scholars do, it's likely not incorrect to say that it is our job to try to recover the work that others sometimes overlook, which is another way of saying that our job is to historicize the things we study—that is, to study things as *human* things. So, for instance, instead of taking the idea of the nation for granted, and thus assume that all human beings ought to identify by means of a nationality (e.g., "I'm Dutch" or "You're Brazilian"), the scholar who studies nationalism would instead be interested in when people first started to organize and identify in this manner; after all, it isn't difficult to study old texts and to see people identifying in rather different ways, often doing so on a far more local basis than the large-scale national identities we now assume ourselves to possess and share with so many others. For such a scholar, the idea of the nation would be seen as the result of human ingenuity and human labor—a way of naming and organizing ourselves that we came up with, that we put in place, and that we continue to reproduce and even tweak. (Have you ever asked yourself why nations develop pledges, flags, and anthems, and then ensure that young children pay close attention to these? There's more work taking place than you might imagine.) This is what we mean by historicizing: not just to place the items we study into historical contexts but also to assume that all things human had beginnings, require constant labor, and will have ends. (No one identifies as Prussian anymore, right?) So, when it comes to people who claim to possess a deep and pre-social experience that is somehow superior to those who unthinkingly participate in mere rituals and ceremonies, in what new ways might we, as scholars, hear or read such claims if we are instead persuaded that all meaning-making—which includes the very fact of responding, "I'm spiritual but not religious"—is the result of being situated within an institution and a tradition?

Well, as suggested near the opening of this chapter, we might come to hear it as not that different from saying "Roll Tide." For in both cases—once we assume all meaning-making is a form of situated, social, and thus collaborative human labor—a limit is being drawn that includes those who identify with this way of talking and this way of conceiving the world which by definition therefore excludes all those who do not. To rephrase, if we assume that all human beings are situated within institutions (though not always the same institutions, of course; and that's a key point—there's a competition taking place), then how might we authorize those we take for granted, those into which we were born or opt to join? And, conversely, how might we de-authorize their competitors; for there's many ways of organizing ourselves socially, politically, economically, and so how will we give those we favor a competitive advantage?

One way is to use rhetoric—to use language to accomplish specific social things.

For example, have you ever heard someone say, "Well, it goes without saying that …"? If whatever they were talking about truly went without saying, then why do they follow up that opening by saying the thing that apparently doesn't have to be said? "It goes without saying that cheetahs are the fastest land animal." We'd suggest that the opening to that sentence is a tactical move in what is actually a debate, though the speaker is working very hard to stop the debate before it even starts. For if "everybody knows" something or if "it's commonsense that …", then it's unlikely that someone present will challenge the point, since by doing so they risk falling well outside the circle of the common and the everybody who apparently knows otherwise (according to the speaker). The claim, then, can be heard as a way to erase debate by preempting it, by portraying anyone who disagrees as speaking nonsense and therefore falling outside the group. For no one ever says, "It goes without saying that we need to breathe." Why? Because it actually does go without saying—that is, we more than likely don't have to persuade each other to breathe and thus don't debate the merits of breathing. (There is no anti-breathing lobby in government, right?) But when it comes to something debatable, something for which there are multiple viable viewpoints—like the meaning of *Ciao*, perhaps?—those with something at stake in the debate may try to advance their claim strategically, and one way to do that is to portray your knowledge as being beyond debate. "Because everybody knows . . .."

Or another technique is trying to erase the history of your claim—present it as self-evident and thus always apparent to everyone; for it likely doesn't help those who, say, wish to portray the nation as an inevitable unit of social organization to have it pointed out that nations are really not that old and that human beings organized themselves socially in far different ways for far longer (e.g., kinship groups or tribes), long before the modern nation-state came along in the nineteenth century. (Depending when your ancestors arrived, they likely didn't have passports; they just got on ships and walked ashore somewhere new.) Or, not too differently, you may opt to create the impression of self-evidency by erasing the institutions in which you learned this or that piece of information. "Everybody knows ..." is one way to do that, for now it's not just people of a certain class or gender who ought to know something, or those who went to certain schools or worked in certain industries, but apparently everyone, regardless of their situation. And, if we're working with that popular (but, as we've argued, flawed) model of meaning-making, we might make this very move by positing a pre-institutional and thus private and therefore deeply personal insight, one that doesn't result from students and teachers working within structures, people who were taught by yet others who were themselves working within structures (like the structures of language or the structure of the educational system) but that, instead, spontaneously springs to your mind (or your heart). Doesn't that sound like a pretty effective way to prioritize one position in an ongoing debate and portray it as something other than one among many options? For the result is that we now have the truly lone, rugged individual, on the one hand, who possesses spontaneous, universal wisdom, and on the other, those who participate in unthinking institutions, following the unoriginal lead of others.

Applications to claims of being "spiritual but not religious"

As we said before, if heard with a critical ear, SBNR claims can now be understood as evidence of an arm wrestling match; it's a strategic move to sanction one social situation, over all others, by positing the existence of a nonnegotiable core to our being that was there before institutions were invented.

But, as also argued here, the very language in which SBNR claims are being made, or even the assumption that people have spirits, is itself evidence of an elaborate tradition, with institutions of its own, that stretches back centuries is an irony we best not recognize if we're intent on not troubling such claims. (Case in point: no one today decided on their own that "spirit" was a good word for the supposedly non-corporeal basis to the human, did they?) But if, we noted earlier, we're scholars—scholars who seek to historicize the human things that we study—then we can't help but be curious about anyone who claims to supersede the social and the institutional (such as someone who fails to understand that, as soon as they say the word "spirituality," they've marked themselves as part of a specific social and linguistic tradition). And this curiosity may lead us to ask some questions about why people today even engage in this sort of talk (curious about what arm wrestling matches they're engaged in), wondering why those institutions called churches, and which were once seen to be of such central importance to society that virtually everyone belonged to one, are now sites from which some people wish to distinguish themselves. What is it about our age that prompts some members of our society to understand themselves as existing apart from it, despite using the same language, economic system, and so forth as those from whom they feel alienated? These are questions worth pursuing, and who knows in what direction such a pursuit will take you, but they're questions that are only possible if we rethink the common assumptions that seem to drive those SBNR claims—assumptions about the pre-social or even asocial nature of just some ways of being in the world. For if we instead start from the standpoint that it's, well ..., standpoint all the way down and that there is nowhere to stand that isn't situated, that isn't invested, that isn't implicated, that isn't part of a prior conversation that we didn't start ourselves, and that isn't therefore part of a social and thus institutional world, then those who talk as if their private, true, or authentic self somehow trumps the so-called derivative forms that other people's lives take will be seen by us as fascinating players in an ongoing contest, working with what's at hand, to give their position a competitive edge.

8

"Learning about religion leads to tolerance"

Tenzan Eaghll

On November 17, 2015, a week after a terrorist attack in Paris that killed 130 people, then-presidential US Republican candidate John Kasich called for the creation of a new federal agency to promote "Judeo-Christian Western values" and improve religious tolerance on a global scale. Quite explicitly, he drew a connection between the Judeo-Christian tradition and an education in the liberal "values of democracy, freedom of speech, freedom of religion, and freedom of association" (Collins 2015). Echoing an old colonialist mindset, Kasich seemed to suggest that the best values are Western values and that if we are going to defeat terrorism we must draw on these ideals as a resource. Now, from a certain angle, what Kasich suggested was simply an attempt to console those who were suffering in the wake of an unspeakable tragedy committed in the name of "religion." However, from another angle, his assertions expose the assumption in the West that learning the truth about religion is the necessary step for improving tolerance and mutual understanding on a global scale, and that the model for doing so is inherently Judeo-Christian.

In this chapter, I will tease out the historical and scholarly origins of this idea, which rely on a theological and clichéd view of religious education. As we will see, the desire to form an agency to promote Judeo-Christian

Western values reflects a very old European project and is deeply connected to what Timothy Fitzgerald calls "the ideology of religious studies." Since the sixteenth century, the cliché that learning the truth about religion will improve tolerance and mutual understanding has both informed popular representations about religion and contributed to the rise of religious studies as an academic discipline (compare, for example, to Jennifer Eyl's chapter on how "religion makes people moral" in this volume). To demonstrate the point, I will begin by tracing the historical and philosophical assumptions underlying this cliché and then discuss its academic formation and contemporary use. I will focus largely on the work of Ninian Smart, as he is one of the first scholars who advanced an apparently nonreligious or secular form of religious education to establish a universal understanding of religion, but will also discuss some of his theological forerunners and modern critics. Overall, I will suggest that the approach to religious education espoused by educators and politicians influenced by Smart and his forerunners is clichéd because it presents itself as theologically and politically neutral, even though it is clearly a remnant of old European Christian ecumenicism. I will point out that this Judeo-Christian, theological, and value-laden approach to the subject seeks to define religion according to its various social dimensions while simultaneously trying to isolate something transcendent about religion that goes well beyond its historical aspects. Although this might be a valid way to approach the topic in a church, Sunday school setting, or perhaps even at a political rally, it should not be the purpose of the academic study of religion.

Christian ecumenical origins

Ecumenism—the attempt to foster tolerance and mutual understanding between religious groups—is not a new endeavor dreamed up by modern politicians and educators but can be traced back to some of the earliest theories of religion. Between the sixteenth and seventeenth centuries thinkers such as Jean Bodin, Baruch Spinoza, and Edward Herbert of Cherbury also advanced a similar idea. These thinkers were writing before "religious studies" existed as an independent academic discipline in universities, and thus the fundamental context for their work was Christian theology and ecumenical dialogue, yet they fostered a cliché that continues to inspire contemporary theories of religion.

Historically, ecumenicism is the age-old Christian practice of developing close and amicable relationships between different churches, and in the wake of Martin Luther's protest over indulgences in 1517, it became an issue of great importance in Western discourse. The terms "ecumenism" and "ecumenical" come from the Greek word *oikoumene* and were originally connected to the call to teach the gospel "throughout the whole world" in Matthew 24:14, but nothing quite transformed the meaning and implications of this evangelical call like the European Reformation. Prior to the Reformation, "Christianity" consisted of all lands united under the Holy Roman Emperor—what was called "Christendom"—but from 1517 onwards Christianity became a contested term that referred to many differing and competing "faith communities." From 1524 to 1648, for instance, the Wars of Religion plunged Europe into a bloody conflict between Protestants and Catholics that left millions dead.[1] From this point onward, bringing the differing faith communities into dialogue (and, hopefully, agreement) was of central importance for both theologians and philosophers alike, and it is out of this ecumenical search to overcome political and cultural differences that our modern understanding of religion emerges.[2] While privileging religion as a unique form of culture distinct from other aspects of culture—such as music, law, or philosophy—theorists advanced a generic religious truth that did not depend on denomination-specific dogmatic grounds. Of course this generic religious truth had a lot of Christian assumptions built into it, but these theorists concealed such theological commitments by presenting their ideology as a seemingly non-confessional discourse of religious neutrality.[3] What we find in these developments is not the end of Christendom and the beginning of religiously neutral secular modernity, but, instead, the migration of certain religious beliefs from the confines of the monastery and the church into the domain of academic scholarship and state diplomacy. Henceforth, Christian theological discourses began to be replaced with broader philosophical and political discourses on the universal truth of religion (Bossy 1985, Cavanaugh 2009).[4] It is in this precise manner that the cliché of religious education took shape alongside—and in conjunction with—the formation of early modern political interests.

For instance, in Bodin's treatise, *Colloquium of the Seven regarding the hidden secrets of the sublime things* (1588), he attempts not only to define religion but also to uncover the ultimate theological truth that lies behind sectarian differences. In his book, Bodin places seven sages with differing religious perspectives in conversation to establish what they share in common and then presents these commonalities as the fundamental principles of religion. He starts from the assumption that all religions share a true, common core and then attempts to expose this truth to overcome religious conflict; assuming that if we could see that all religions shared some basic core beliefs, then perhaps we could all get along better. The religious views he represents were quite broad for his day and included a natural philosopher, a Calvinist, a Muslim, a Roman Catholic, a Lutheran, a Jew, and a skeptic. The sages in Bodin's imagined conversation discuss not only the nature of truth but also the political climate that was leading to the Wars of Religion. As the scholar J. Samuel Preus notes, the *Colloquium* offers us one of the first attempts to break with explicitly Jewish or Christian theology and extract the common rationalist principles behind scriptural difference (1987, 3–10).

Similarly, in Spinoza's *Theological Political Treatise* (1670), there is a desire to draw out the fundamental principles behind religious diversity for communal ends; he was also motivated by the wars of religion, and at the beginning of his treatise he explicitly states that his goal is to find a solution to religious violence. Spinoza defines religion as "obedience to the universal moral law and not adherence to any particular confession, faith, or doctrine" and argues that for peace to arise, both worldly and spiritual power must be under the sovereign control of the political order (Spinoza 2007, 49n. 5; 238–49). The worship of God is to be a free and individual affair, but he argues that "[t]he highest form of piety is that which is practiced with respect to the peace and tranquility of the state" (253). In this manner, what thinkers such as Bodin and Spinoza attempted to present is the core essence of religious truth extracted for their particular political ends, and they did so by providing a broad, pluralist definition of religion that would include all of the competing religious groups of their day.

Herbert of Cherbury, who wrote in the seventeenth century, offers a very similar theoretical perspective as Bodin and Spinoza.

As a diplomat, he faced many of the same political circumstances and was also confronted with the challenge of finding peace in an age of conflict. Although Germany had found calm with the Peace of Ausburg (1555), the Wars of Religion of 1618–48 placed the Catholic league against the Protestant Union, so he was also interested in ecumenical dialogue. In Herbert's work, he did not seek the oldest form of religion but its most common principles. In *On Truth, as It Is Distinguished from Revelation, the Probable, the Possible, and the False* (1624), he surveyed the religions that existed in Europe and came up with principles that were supposedly common to all. Prefiguring modern definitions of religion, he suggested that there were five universal principles by which all religions were structured: (1) there is only one God, (2) this God ought to be worshiped, (3) virtue is the chief end of religion, (4) people ought to repent of their sins, and (5) there is life after death. Herbert attempted to extract these principles because he wanted to found true religion upon common notions, just like the practice of law, and thereby bring it under the domain of reason and state legislation (Preus 1987, 23–40).

I mention these early theories of religion in passing to expose the political ambitions at the heart of the Western approach to religious education. The contemporary understanding of the topic, as it relates to tolerance and mutual understanding, is deeply connected to the theological attempt to incorporate Judeo-Christian notions into state ideologies. It took shape when theologians and philosophers began projecting their own idea of "God" and the "sacred" on other cultures and communities in an attempt to bring these differing peoples into dialogue and under a common law. In the sixteenth century this desire was expressed in an attempt to calm the wars between Catholics and Protestants, and in the twenty-first century between Islam and the West, but the use of religious education to overcome these conflicts conceals a similar theological imperative. As Timothy Fitzgerald notes, the word "religion" is "so thoroughly imbued with Judeo-Christian monotheistic associations" that it colors all modern connotations ascribed to it (Fitzgerald 2000, 19). Of course, there is nothing intrinsically wrong with attempting to resolve societal conflicts with theology, but we should be aware of the ideological and political commitments or biases concealed within the solutions we offer.

Between the seventeenth and the nineteenth centuries, theorists expanded the scope and breadth of the definitions of religion provided by Bodin, Spinoza, and Herbert, but they weren't entirely able to break with this confessional association between education and religion. From the vast historical accounts of the development of religion in the work of Bernard Fontenelle and Giambattista Vico, to the empirical and rationalistic accounts of religion in the work of David Hume and Immanuel Kant, there remained a theological agenda that legitimized Western views of religion. Rather than critiquing problematic Western assumptions about religion, these thinkers universalized them as human features shared by all rational beings, spreading a cultural ethnocentrism that privileged a European view of the world, a project that was tied to the imperialistic interests of Western governments—European nations often justified colonialism in part by arguing that people in those cultures who did not exhibit these Christian values were not fully rational. Indeed, even in the work of anthropologists and sociologists like Edward Tylor, James Frazer, and Émile Durkheim—who were the first to analyze religion as something invented by humans rather than the gods—there remained an unquestioned reliance on Judeo-Christian notions and distinctions. These theorists, sympathetic to the so-called primitive cultures they studied, depicted and distorted them in their own image, finding evidence for God and the sacred in aboriginal tribes from Australia to the Amazon (Preus 1987).

In fact, up until the late 1950s, religious instruction in the West was still directly tied to the church. As Ninian Smart notes in his memoirs, when he went to Oxford the study of religion existed only within "divinity schools and University Departments of Theology in State schools" (1998a, 18). Until this period, it was possible to learn about the comparative study of religion in theological schools but not under the direction of the non-theological social and human sciences, a fact that was true in Australia, South Africa, America, and all European countries. In Britain, for instance, it was simply assumed that the church was a positive element of the education system and that training students to be knowledgeable about the world was intertwined with training them to be good Christians. Students were expected to not only get good grades but also become better religious servants for the state (Barnes 2000, 316). For instance, the Cambridge Agreed Syllabus of 1949 states that its educational goal is "to lead children to an experience of God, His Church, and His Word, an experience based on worship, fellowship and service" (Cox 1983, 30). In this manner, political, educational, and theological interests have long been linked in the West.

Modern developments

The radical economic, social, and intellectual transformations that swept across the Western world in the 1960s created a climate that made possible the reassessment of this traditional approach to religious education, and Smart was at the forefront of this movement. He helped set up the Department of Religious Studies at Lancaster University, which pioneered the subject in its full form for all Commonwealth countries (Smart 1998a, 19). In *The Teacher and Christian Belief* (1966) and *Secular Education and the Logic of Religion* (1968), Smart laid out a specific model for religious education by incorporating the social sciences to the study of religion, suggesting that only through a liberal understanding of the subject can the modern state promote cultural tolerance. Arguing against the traditional method of teaching theology, he suggested that what is needed in our increasingly pluralist and secular world is not instruction in religious belief but neutral instruction in religious diversity. What I want to propose in this section is that, although Smart does make strides in the direction of religiously neutral critical research, he does not go far enough and ends up passing off the old Christian ecumenical project as if it were a religiously neutral, secular discourse.

In *The Teacher and Christian Belief,* for instance, which was Smart's first book on the topic, his tone is deeply theological despite the fact that he tries to expand religious education beyond its strictly confessional borders. At this early point in Smart's career, he suggests that a broad religious education is the best way to initiate students into the truth about the subject, yet he also claims that Christianity is a unique revealed religion. Tellingly, he suggests that by simply teaching students Christian dogma they grow skeptical, but if you teach them a "broad religious outlook," they will come to these revealed—that is, Christian—truths on their own (1966, 140).

Two years later when Smart published *Secular Education and the Logic of Religion,* his position was far more nuanced and critical, yet still deeply linked to Christian theology. He describes the old theological approach to religious education as schizophrenic because it closes theology in on itself and divides the student between the secular and the religious (1968, 90–1). To counter this approach, he suggests that what is needed is a new non-theological way to study religion that opens Christian doctrine and Biblical revelation to the "wider world of philosophy and history." Specifically, he argues that the study of religion in the modern world cannot be dogmatic: "It must introduce, even from out of its own substance, the sympathetic appreciation of positions and faiths other than its own. Christian theology, in brief, must be open, not closed" (1968, 90–1). Since the different forms of religion share some fundamental similarities across different cultures, their distinctive patterns and dimensions must be studied.

Smart's approach to religious education was transformational because it added a new social and material element to the old Christian ecumenicalism. By institutionalizing the idea that the truths of religion are constituted by, not in competition with, cultural difference, he argued that the comparable worlds of myth, ritual, and doctrine are the higher universal truth of both Christianity and other traditions and that education needs to reflect this truth. From a certain angle, this did away with much of the Christian-specific theology that underlay the old theories of religion by universalizing Western notions about God and the sacred. However, from another angle, it was the same old Christian ecumenicalism but posited on a global scale.[5] Smart concludes his study with five theses that summarize his position and its goals:

First, religious education should transcend the informative. Second, it should do so not in the direction of evangelizing, but in the direction of initiation into understanding the meaning of, and into questions about the truth and worth of, religion. Third, religious studies do not exclude a committed approach provided that it is open, and so does not artificially restrict understanding and choice. Fourth, religious studies should provide a service in helping people to understand history and other cultures than our own. It can thus play a vital role in breaking the limits of European cultural tribalism. Fifth, religious studies should emphasize the descriptive, historical side of religion, but need thereby to enter into dialogue with the parahistorical claims of religious and anti-religious outlooks. (Smart 1968, 106)

Note how he attempts to locate religion within a historical and cultural description of phenomena while also preserving its transcendent and nonhistorical aspects (i.e., those parts of a tradition that transcended material reality). Smart is attempting to provide a new historical method for achieving the aims of the old Christian ecumenical project.

For instance, in 1972 when Smart penned the article, "Comparative Religion Clichés: Crushing the Clichés about Comparative Religion and then Accentuating the Positive Value of the New Religious Education," his goal was to advance a new model for religious education. He wanted to do away with the old theological clichés that served as the foundation of confessional instruction in Europe since the Middle Ages and usher in a new objective approach to the study of religion, one which would foster tolerance and understanding on a global scale. In this article, Smart drew a distinction between denominational and secular religious instruction and suggested that in today's world what was needed was an "'open-ended' religious education" that was not concerned with dogma but only an "initiation into understanding." What interested him, he stated, was not indoctrination into Christianity but the more general "meaning of religion and religions" (1972, 6). Or, as Smart put it in 1987 when discussing "The Political Implications of Religious Studies," he wanted to establish a "federalism of tolerance" that "allows individuals and groups great freedoms to choose the worldviews that they will live by" (1987, 46).

In his many publications spanning over thirty years, Smart attempted to achieve this new understanding of religious education by (1) defining religion in universal terms and (2) linking this definition with a new global ethic of tolerance. First, in his many works Smart developed a phenomenological approach that helped facilitate the rise of the academic study of religion. By isolating the elementary aspects of all cultural worldviews he suggested that monotheistic, polytheistic, and even atheistic traditions could be shown to exhibit several fundamental religious traits. In 1967, Smart formalized this into what he called the six *dimensions of religion*, but in his later work he added a seventh: doctrinal, mythical, ethical, experiential, ritual, institutional, and material (Smart 1998a, 23–4).[6] These seven dimensions of religion are a classification schema meant to ensure that scholarly treatments of religion are balanced, are objective, and reflect the multidisciplinary nature of religious studies, while simultaneously suggesting that the broader truth of religious phenomena is not reducible to any one of them.

Recall that the English term "phenomenology" (*Phänomenologie*) is a uniquely German invention. It comes from a combination of the Greek word *logos* (word, reason, theory, etc.) and *phainomenon* (appearance) and implies "the study of that which appears." Protestant theologians in the twentieth century such as Rudolf Otto and Gerardus Van der Leeuw applied phenomenology to religion and argued that there are mystical experiences of "the holy" (*Das Heilige*), which they claimed exists outside the material world and cannot be understood with rational concepts. These theologians suggested that if the material world is the domain of empirical conscious experience, then the holy is the domain of transcendental conscious experience. In this manner, they argued that religion provides access to a unique (*sui generis*) domain of human experience that lies beyond the confines of everyday worldly knowledge (see Otto 1958, Van der Leeuw 2014). In turn, Smart appropriated this phenomenological methodology but argued that this experience of the holy, or the "numinous"—from the Latin *numen,* meaning "divine power"—has various social dimensions that can be studied in all human cultures. By organizing religions according to their doctrinal, mythical, ethical, experiential, ritual, institutional, and material elements, he provided a potentially theoretically neutral method for studying the historical appearances of something that presumably transcended history.

As Russell McCutcheon notes, what makes Smart's definition of religion phenomenological is that he organized religion according to "aspects or family of traits that typified religions" (2007, 172). By compartmentalizing the numinous into the various cultural elements in which it appeared, Smart could assert that he was moving away from the traditional confessional approach to religion and that numinous religious experiences could be studied crossculturally. However, this ended up preserving the theological essence of the confessional approach to religious education in a new "descriptive" and "historical" scientific language (Smart 1998a, 22).[7] At the end of the day, Smart doesn't actually investigate religion but merely passes the buck, so to speak, and declares that religion is produced by a series of dimensions that are defined *as* religious.

Second, Smart consistently suggested that these dimensions of religion are the best way of dealing with cultural difference in contemporary society and linked his definition of religion with the higher moral and spiritual truth of all humanity (1987, 46). He repeatedly pointed to the similar ethical injunctions in Buddhism, Hinduism, Islam, Christianity, and even Maoist communism to suggest that all religions were directed toward similar ethical commands and that, if properly understood, these imperatives could be channeled toward a new global ethic. Smart wanted to unite phenomenology and global plurality to develop new "tolerant attitudes, which in a world perspective imply certain religious attitudes." In this light, his new approach to religious education was meant to advance "empathy," minimize violence, and advance "a sense of universal world citizenship" (1998b, 332).

Combining these two points together, we might summarize the basis of Smart's new religious education as an attempt to uncover the deeper phenomenological truth of reality in the values of empathy, tolerance, and understanding. He argued that learning about the various dimensions of religion was not simply about accumulating data—that is, not simply memorizing how Muslims, Buddhists, and Taoists live their lives—but creating moral individuals. In his various essays and books he constantly links religious teachings with this cultivation of empathy. As he writes, the role of religious education in the university is to cultivate a community of spiritual equanimity:

> [T]hough Buddhist values such as the great *brahmaviharas* [loving-kindness, compassion, empathy, equanimity] are primarily aimed at the cultivation of fine and upright individuals and to help them in their process of spiritual betterment, they also are relevant to the creation of objectivity and empathy in the scholarly community. I think the true student of the humanities and the social sciences in particular should value equanimity and the practice of *sati* [skillful awareness]. This is where there is a bonding between religious values and the pursuit of higher education. (1998b, 309)

With this argument, Smart is suggesting that through a thorough study of religious diversity we learn tolerance and mutual understanding. He is suggesting that the specific dimensions of religion teach these empathetic qualities and that this is the goal of religious education. As his emphasis on the Buddhist practice of *sati* exposes, he sees the study of religion as an education in empathy and compassion and, like his Protestant forerunners, wants to use theological truths for the betterment of the world. Even though he presents his methodology as a historical and social scientific analysis of religion, he sees its ultimate end as a moral way of relating to experiences of something transcendent.

In sum, what makes Smart's approach to religious education a cliché is that he universalizes the old theological assumptions of Christian ecumenicism in the name of social scientific research. He presents his approach to the "dimensions of religion" as an objective study of phenomena and suggests that a sustained study of these dimensions instructs students in the truth of religion and transforms them into ethical subjects, which is, at bottom, a theological project cloaked in a secular guise. As he writes, "if we were to cultivate the virtues which arise from the whole enterprise of pursuing the truth, we would have a splendid ethic to present to our students and even the outside world" (1993, 135). It is in this sense, as Donald Wiebe once quipped, "Smart's own work seems to contribute to a view of religious studies as a religious exercise" (2005, 109). By arguing that the higher truth of religion is irreducible to any particular theological doctrine, political setting, or sociological context, Smart is attempting to put religion to work for the betterment of the modern state. He is not just concerned with exploring the meaning of religion at a discursive and textual level—examining what people say about religion at a social scientific level—but extracting its core truth for the betterment of the world. Of course, doing theology is fine, in and of itself, but we should not present theological scholarship as an objective study of historical facts. To do so not only obscures the political and historical origins of religion in the West but also serves a latent ideological function. The latter may be a valuable goal in a seminary school or a church, but it should not be the point of the academic study of religion.

Popular success and critique

The success of Smart's developments and their influence on religious studies cannot be understated, though he should not be single-handedly credited with this ecumenical achievement—which, as we have seen, stretches back centuries. In the 1980s and 1990s his phenomenological method and his emphasis on a federalism of tolerance became the norm for the subject. In the 1995 *Agreed Syllabus for Religious Education* (England and Wales), the Christian Education Movement used this phenomenological methodology to define how religious educators are to teach the subject. Religious education, it suggests, is henceforth to be a positive search for the meaning and purpose of life that is "common to all human beings" (Templeton 1999, 75–6).[8] To date, many universities in North America have accepted this methodological approach rather unproblematically. Although there are many critics of this paradigm, they are often in the minority in any given department. A simple search online reveals many conferences, books, courses, television programs, and politicians that associate religious education with an improved sense of tolerance and mutual understanding.

For instance, in 2016 Harvard's Divinity School began offering a free online course to the general public that follows this paradigm. The course seeks to improve tolerance and understanding about religion by improving religious literacy. Titled Religious Literacy: Traditions and Scriptures, the course includes six classes on different topics and will be followed by more specific courses on Christianity, Buddhism, Islam, Hinduism, and Judaism. Although the course pretends to be theoretically innovative, it is actually just a repackaging of the old "seven dimensions" model established by Smart. For starters, the Web site states that, "[t]he study of religion is the study of a rich and fascinating dimension of human experience that includes but goes well beyond beliefs and ritual practices." Just like Smart, who identified religion as a unique and transcendent aspect of human experience and claimed that it has various social dimensions that can be studied crossculturally, the course designers at Harvard have provided an empirical basis for studying non-empirical phenomena. They have preserved the confessional approach to religious education in apparently scientific language. The core objectives of the course are to teach learners (1) that religions are internally diverse, (2) how they evolve and change through time, and (3) how religions are embedded in all dimensions of human experience. It is important to note how they simultaneously suggest that religions do not function in isolation from their political, economic, and cultural contexts yet still claim that it is impossible to understand a culture without considering its religious dimensions—implying that some part of religion transcends material culture. As we have seen, this classic phenomenological move attempts to define religion by its ordinary cultural aspects that can be studied scientifically, while simultaneously isolating something—the holy or the numinous—that goes well beyond them (Moore and Mudd 2016).

Of course, by incorporating the social and material elements into their definition of religion, courses like this are certainly an improvement on the overtly theological analysis of the subject that characterized the Cambridge Agreed Syllabus of 1949, but by failing to submit the category itself to analysis, they continue to present religion as a unique domain of human experience that is not reducible to any social scientific category. After all, if religion and culture are inseparable, how are they able to refer to religion as something unique that exceeds or transcends the limits of human practice? In the vein of Smart, the course designers at Harvard seek to create a federalism of tolerance that conceals a theological agenda in an apparently secular guise.

At the more general level of popular culture, examples of this cliché are even more rampant than those found in books and free online courses on the subject. Numerous Web sites and television events have been constructed to connect education, religion, and cultural tolerance and understanding. One of the most successful attempts to embody this message was Joseph Campbell's well-received PBS special, *The Power of Myth* (1988), which everyone who had a TV during the 1980s seems to have watched. The show presented religious difference as an opportunity to understand the higher truth about human existence, and it offered this understanding by educating the general public in the truth about religion and myth.

More recently, Oprah Winfrey has also jumped into the fray and funded a television program called *Belief* (2015), which first appeared on the Discovery Channel and is now available online. Oprah's series combines ethnographic imagery of religious activities from around the world set according to themes like practice, faith, the good life, and so forth. Oprah's *Belief* blends all religious difference together in a universal interpretation of human culture, while simultaneously trying to isolate what goes beyond them. Interestingly enough, it was also Smart who popularized this medium of religious education. In the late 1970s Smart teamed up with the BBC to create a television program called *The Long Search* (1977), which surveyed the major religions of the world according to his theory of religious dimensions. Looking at the different forms of Christianity, Buddhism, Islam, Judaism, Hinduism, and New Age movements, Smart's program provided an introduction to religion for the general public that attempted to demonstrate the universal truth of religion behind cultural difference.

As noted in the introduction to this chapter, this cliché has also impacted popular political discourse. The previous example was US Republican presidential candidate John Kasich's plan for the creation of a new federal agency to promote Judeo-Christian Western values. However, examples could also be drawn from Presidents George W. Bush and Barack Obama, as both have also linked religious education to the spread of modern liberal values. For instance, on December 10, 2009, Obama accepted the Nobel Peace Prize and connected a proper understanding of religion to the spread of liberal values in our modern secular world. Drawing a distinction between particular religious identities and universal religious experience, Obama suggested that a true understanding of religion requires that we leave behind the particular, tribal, and local concerns in the name of a universal faith that is the absolute truth of all religions. Asserting that this understanding of religion is "the law of love [that] has always been the core struggle of human nature," he suggests that adhering to this truth and acting according to it is the only way to honor the "spark of the divine that still stirs within each of our souls" (Obama 2009). As I have been suggesting, this might be a valid way to approach the topic in a church, Sunday school setting, and perhaps even at a political rally, but insofar as it appeals to transcendent matters not subject to empirical or historical investigation, it needs to be distinguished from the academic study of religion.

As Fitzgerald argues, this value-laden approach to the subject does not help us understand the complexity of the world we live in, but merely functions as a theological tool to separate religion from other aspects of culture, preserving its transcendent claims in a discourse of irreducible phenomenological neutrality. Historically, it is a product of Protestant ideology and tied to the wider historical process of Western imperialism, colonialism, and neocolonialism that this ideology supported. As evidenced by the comments of Kasich and Obama, this is a project that is still alive and well: it functions to advance political interests all the while belying or obscuring its Judeo-Christian ecumenical origins. The theory that the dimensions of religion can be used for the benefit of religious education is therefore perhaps the biggest cliché of all, for it presents itself as theologically neutral, all the while functioning to sustain various political interests in our modern world. Fitzgerald frames this argument in the following terms, summing up much of what I have discussed in this essay:

> The construction of "religion" and "religions" is therefore part of a historical ideological process ... the invention of the modern concept of religion and religions is the correlate of the modern ideology of individualism and capitalism. This ideological product was assumed to have its analogue in colonial cultures, and if religions could not be found then they were invented, along with western individuals, law courts, free markets, and educational systems. "Religion" was part of the complex process of establishing the naturalness and ideological transparency of capitalist and individualist values. The industry known as religious studies is a kind of generating plant for a value laden view of the world that claims to identify religions and faiths as an aspect of all societies and that, by so doing, makes possible another separate "non-religious" conceptual space, a fundamental area of presumed factual objectivity. (2000, 8)

It is for the previous reasons that the study of religion should arguably be reconfigured as the study of religion as an ideological category. Rather than engaging in a pursuit to heal a broken world, the scholar of religion should analyze the categorization, identification, and power associations at work in the use of the term. Instead of trying to secure a tolerant representation of religion, the scholar should teach students how to survey the discursive field at play in any given setting and expose the rules by which religion is defined. In the end, this provides a more potent critique of religion than anything Smart ever dreamed up because it refuses to engage in the debate over what true religion or true theology consists of and focuses on how religion is put to work rhetorically and politically to achieve various ends. Instead of advocating veiled theological clichés in the name of liberal secular truths, it exposes how religion operates in society. As Fitzgerald puts it, "[m]y proposal then is that those of us who work within the so-called field of religion but who reject the domination of ecumenical theology and phenomenology reconceptualize our field of study in such a way that we become critically aligned with theoretical and methodological fields such as anthropology, history, and cultural studies" (2000, 9). Hence, contra Smart, who tried to overcome the old theological clichés of the past with a value-oriented approach to the subject that privileges tolerance and mutual understanding as the key benefits of religious education, I would suggest that the only way to overcome the clichés associated with religious education is to study religion as an ideological category.

Conclusion

Stated simply, the cliché of religious education emerges when it is assumed that the goal of the study of religion is to improve tolerance and understanding about religion, rather than an analysis of its use and function in society. From early modern theorists of religion such as Jean Bodin and Herbert of Cherbury, to the development of the academic study of religion in the twentieth century, this ecumenical aim has formed the ideological core of theories on the topic. In this chapter I have primarily focused on the work of Smart because he is one of the first to popularize this approach. By disguising a value-laden conception of the world in the objective study of social facts, Smart paved the way for the assent of this cliché in academic institutions and popular culture. Through an emphasis on tolerance and mutual understanding, he presented the key benefit of religious education as a lesson in empathy and furthered the transfer of sacred authority from the church to the state. Like Kasich's call for the creation of a new federal agency to promote Judeo-Christian Western values, this approach to religious education does the work of old European Christian ecumenicism at the political level: it spreads Judeo-Christian values in the form of a broad definition of religion that is irreducible to its historical dimensions. In contrast, what is needed is critical analysis of religion and its ideological functions.

9

"Everyone has a faith"

James Dennis LoRusso

S hortly after completing my doctorate in August 2014, I attended
the annual meeting of the Academy of Management (AOM),
the professional society for scholars broadly interested in the
study of management. To say the least, as a scholar of religion in
contemporary America, I felt a little out of my element among a
group primarily dedicated to helping organizations effectively
manage employees. However, my research explores the role of
religion in the workplace, and I was excited at the opportunity to
take part in a group of panels dealing with this very topic, aptly titled
Management, Spirituality, and Religion (MSR). According to the AOM
Web site, the MSR group "explores how spirituality and religion
can influence organizational dynamics and affect management
outcomes" (Academy of Management n.d.). In layman's terms, it
brings together scholars that examine the impact of religion and
spirituality, broadly conceived, on business.

During one of the panels, I was struck when a presenter casually
remarked, "everyone has a faith of some kind." While I strongly
disagreed with his words, what surprised me the most was how
they drew almost no reaction from anyone in the audience, as if
the truth of this idea was so apparent that it warranted no further
explanation. Feeling somewhat duty bound to address the issue,
I raised a hand and politely stated my objection that some people
might take issue with his claim that everyone has a faith. "What

do you mean?" he asked looking confused. "Well," I continued, "I have a number of friends who identify as atheists that might feel somewhat misrepresented by such a statement. What would you say to someone like this who claims no faith at all?" Without blinking, the presenter immediately responded, "I would say atheism *is* their faith. Just as some people place their faith in science, in government, or even in themselves. But, as I said, we all have faith in something," at which point the audience seemed ready to move on, so I dropped the discussion.

Much to my consternation, the exchange stuck with me in the days that followed. I just couldn't seem to pinpoint exactly what troubled me. At first, I thought—correctly I should add—that he was simply confusing two ways of using the word *faith*. While "faith" can refer to a generic devotion to anything (faith in one's family, etc.), it can also connote a specifically *religious* devotion (e.g., "the Christian faith," etc.). After more reflection, however, I realized that the problem was more profound. This idea—everyone has a faith of some kind—deeply permeates American culture. It constitutes a cliché, a stereotype that all of us encounter at various times in our daily interactions.

A cliché can be many things, but typically it is a single word or a short phrase that carries with it some important cultural information beyond its literal meaning. Statements such as "the grass is always greener on the other side" or "when pigs fly" make little sense on their own. After all, pigs don't have wings and in my second-story apartment, I have no lawn. Still, when I hear these phrases in a particular context, I intuitively just *get* their meaning. Essentially, clichés act as a kind of shorthand, a concise statement packed full of emotion and meaning that would otherwise require much more elaboration. We need clichés precisely because they allow us to communicate more efficiently and colorfully.

While effective from a practical standpoint, they nonetheless impose constraints on our thinking. For clichés to work properly, they require us to have some measure of fluency with the cultural context in which they are used. I have to know, for instance, that pigs are animals that cannot fly to deduce that the phrase "when pigs fly" means that a certain state of affairs will never occur. However, if I've never seen a pig, how would I know this? Most of us probably don't consider all of the assumptions contained within a single cliché, and while pigs obviously don't fly on their own, many other clichés, particularly those discussed in this volume, don't always rest on such solid ground. Clichés of this kind convey their meaning by playing on various biases that we simply take for granted. They conform to religion scholar Bruce Lincoln's definition of a myth: *ideology in narrative form* (Lincoln 1999, 147). Clichés, like myths, take certain assumptions about the world as if they are objectively true. Nonetheless, if we take the time to uncover these assumptions and interrogate their validity, we might just glimpse the real cultural power hidden behind the cliché.

In this chapter, we will unpack the seemingly innocuous statement, "everyone has a faith of some kind," and consider how its problematic, underlying assumptions masquerade as self-evident truth. After mapping out a few of these assumptions, we will examine how scholars of religion and theologians have perpetuated them over the course of the twentieth century. In particular, I focus on the work of James Fowler, a theology professor who employs psychology to construct a model for how faith develops over the course of an individual's life. Last, we will turn to popular culture to illustrate briefly how these assumptions get reinforced through the popular science fiction franchise, *Star Trek*.

Hidden assumptions of the cliché

At first glance, it seems rather uncontroversial to suggest that "everyone has some kind of faith." After all, having faith in something is nearly identical to believing in something, and I suspect most people will agree that they hold certain beliefs. Still, more so than belief, faith invokes ideas frequently associated with religious traditions and therefore conveys a kind of wholeness. In fact, American English speakers often substitute *faith* for *religion*. When public figures, for example, speak about "people of faith," they refer not to just any system of belief but to religious adherents specifically; Christianity is dubbed the "Christian Faith," and the White House's Office of Faith-Based and Neighborhood Partnerships, founded by President George W. Bush in 2001, enlists religious organizations in the provision of social services.

References to faith are not merely assertions about belief; they are assertions about *religious* belief.

If classifying a set of beliefs as a faith is akin to calling it religious, then the suggestion that "everyone has a faith of some kind" implies that almost any set of ideas can qualify as a religion. Thus the presenter at the AOM meeting who labeled atheism and science as faiths was, at least potentially, intimating not only that they are no different from other religions but also ultimately that science and atheism are essentially religious. This gets us to our first hidden assumption:

Assumption one: All belief, ideologies, or worldviews are basically expressions of faith.

This first premise leads directly to the second assumption. Because everyone presumably subscribes to some kind of belief, ideology, or worldview, then faith is universal. Faith comprises part of our nature; to be human is to be a person of faith.

Assumption two: Faith is a universal aspect of human experience.

Even if we posit that human beings possess some innate capacity called faith, its expressions would necessarily vary over time and space. Everyone may have a faith, but it is a faith of some particular kind. Although the historical religious traditions may shape its outward manifestation, faith is wholly private, emerging from within the individual.

Assumption three: Religion is an outward expression of individual, private faith.

All three assumptions are circulating in the claim that "everyone has some kind of faith." For the cliché to make sense, we must assume that faith is innate to human nature, is unique to each individual, and informs every belief that we hold about the world. By revealing these hidden assumptions, however, we can begin to expose their rather problematic qualities. Collapsing all views under the category of faith obscures the differences between what are, in reality, a diverse set of perspectives and experiences. Arguably, referring to all belief systems as faiths grossly misrepresents many religious and nonreligious perspectives alike. Does a Tibetan Buddhist have "faith" in the sense used here? Would a climate scientist equate the scientific theories upon which her work is based to the faith of the Catholic Church? If not, on what grounds can we classify all of these perspectives under the label "faith?" Finally, if we cannot be certain that each of these are faiths, then how can we justify the claim that faith is innate to all human beings? No matter how obvious the cliché may appear at first glance, it ultimately lacks any solid foundation. Yet, as we shall see throughout the remainder of this chapter, these assumptions continue to inform scholarship on religion and American culture more generally.

Inventing "faith" as human nature

Although we lack the space in this chapter to provide an adequate history on the very idea of faith, we can briefly survey how this concept emerged out of Protestant Christianity and how twentieth-century scholarship has perpetuated the three assumptions undergirding the cliché that everyone has some kind of faith.

The English word *faith* evolved from the Latin root *Fides*, which roughly translates as *belief* or *trust*, and was not necessarily associated with religious belief during pre-Christian Rome. Instead, *fides* meant something like *reliability* or *legitimate*, a meaning that we can still recognize in English words like bona*fide*, *fide*lity, and even proper names like Fidel (as in the late Cuban leader Fidel Castro) or the name of one's dog (i.e., Fido). Faith, however, took on a specific theological understanding with the spread of Christianity during the late Roman Empire in the first few centuries CE. Faith, according to early Christian thinkers and scriptures, was integral to Christian beliefs. As the Letter to the Hebrews in the New Testament states, "without faith it impossible to please [God], for whoever would draw near to God must believe that he exists and that he rewards those who seek him" (Heb. 11:6, ESV). Here, we can still recognize the pre-Christian sense of faith as reliability—having faith in God means a willingness to trust him to reward a believer. Yet, for Christian thinkers, faith meant something more than having trust; it represented an essential ingredient for the salvation of one's soul.

The schism between the Roman Catholics and Protestants that began during the sixteenth century further intensified the theological significance of faith. Whereas the Catholic Church generally accepted (as it does today) faith as one part of the Christian life alongside reason and action, Protestant thinkers like Martin Luther argued that faith alone (*sola fide*) embodies the very foundation of all human knowledge of God and the motivation behind all truly Christian acts. In other words, the single most important element of Christianity was faith and therefore, in the Protestant sense, to be religious was to have faith.

In rendering faith and religion as identical concepts, Protestants diminished the importance of the church and essentially reconceived faith as a private affair between God and individual believers, between Christ and the "faithful." People, they presumed, have no need for church guidance because they already possess an innate capacity for faith without the creeds, priests, or hierarchy of the Catholic Church. In the wake of the Protestant Reformation, we might say that Christianity became the Christian faith.

As Western Europe expanded its power across the globe during the modern period, they appealed to this Protestant frame to classify the various beliefs and practices of foreign peoples. If each person exhibits the capacity for faith, then the variation of faiths across the world merely indicate superficial differences overlaying a common core shared by all religions. In the last century, some of the most influential scholars and theologians have appealed to these well-entrenched assumptions in their work.

William James, a pioneering psychologist of religion, crafted his classic study of religious experience around the idea that a common essence could be found linking all expressions of religion. In *The Varieties of Religious Experience* (1902), James differentiated between *institutional* and *personal* religion. While "worship and sacrifice, procedures for working on the dispositions of the deity, theology and ceremony and ecclesiastical organization" exemplified the former,

> in the more personal branch of religion it is on the contrary the inner dispositions of man himself which form the center of interest, his conscience, his deserts, his helplessness, his incompleteness. (James 2002, 34)

Here, James wants to draw our attention to the interior dimensions of religious life, and moreover, he goes even further to suggest that "personal religion will prove itself more fundamental than either theology or ecclesiasticism" (35). Thus, without discounting the role of religious dogma, scripture, and traditions, James declares that religion can only be understood by examining its personal, private dimensions divorced from its historical contexts.

Like James, Rudolf Otto's *The Idea of the Holy* (1917) and later Gerardus Van der Leeuw's *Religion in Essence and Manifestation* (1933) both stressed the essential nature of the religious experience. For Otto, all religion originates with so-called *numinous* experience, a nonrational, indescribable experience of something *wholly other*. It was this experience in which the key—the underlying nature of mankind's religiosity—might be exposed. Van der Leeuw, similarly, locates the essence of religion in the individual's encounter with *the sacred*. Both thinkers suggest that to truly study religion, we must assume the existence of an innate sense of the religious, or perhaps a religious sense that everyone (at least potentially) exhibits. Thinkers like James, Otto, and Van der Leeuw separated religion into its intrinsic and extrinsic components, privileging the former over the latter.

By the mid-twentieth century, this bifurcation between the outward forms of religion and its undifferentiated core was commonplace, setting the stage for two scholars that would begin to refer to the intrinsic aspects of religion as faith. The first one is Paul Tillich, one of the most influential American theologians of the twentieth century. His work contributed to the view that faith, or least the capacity for it, was something innate in everyone. For Tillich, faith represents "the state of being ultimately concerned" (Tillich 1957, 1). Like James's concept of *religious experience*, or Otto's *holy*, faith is irreducible and ineffable. In *Dynamics of Faith*, Tillich writes that "faith precedes all attempts to derive it from something else, because these are themselves based on faith" (8). In short, faith represents the beginning and end of all human knowledge. It is our faith in something, Tillich argues, that allows us to think and act in the world, and moreover it is the realization of our faith to which we ultimately strive. The specific matter with which one is *ultimately concerned* could be anything. Even the heretic and the atheist humanist possess some measure of faith, some kind of ultimate concern, because faith, he suggests, is not strictly "defined as belief in the existence and actions of divine beings" (62). Instead, "if faith is understood as the state of being ultimately concerned about the ultimate, humanism implies faith.... For humanism the divine is manifest in the human; the ultimate concern of man is man" (62). In other words, everyone has a faith of some kind.

Tillich was ultimately a theologian whose ideas must be understood in the context of his religious identity, but others, like Wilfred Cantwell Smith, who were part of the relatively new field of comparative religion were introducing similar ideas about faith to the secular academy. Smith offered one of the first comprehensive critiques of how Western cultures conceived of religion with the publication of *The Meaning and End of Religion* (1962). Smith declared that religion was a grossly inadequate category for capturing the complex and diverse phenomena to which it is typically applied. Calling for a complete reassessment of the field of study, he wrote, "it is perhaps not presumptuous to hold that no definition of religion so far proposed as proven compelling no generalization has come anywhere near to adequacy" (Smith 1962, 11). The problem, Smith argues, lies in the simple fact that religion is not a term that makes much sense in non-Western cultures.

> Man is everywhere and has always been what we today call "religious." Yet there are today and have been in the past relatively few languages into which one can translate the word "religion"— and particularly its plural, "religions"—outside Western civilization. (18)

In short, religion is an idea that originated in the modern West and has only recently been applied (largely by Europeans) to the myriad of culturally specific ideas, philosophies, and practices observed (again, by Europeans) across the world. For instance, Smith calls Hinduism "a particularly false conceptualization" that was imposed from the outside, first by Muslim conquers and later perpetuated by Europeans.

Ultimately, Smith's answer to this problem is to split religion into two distinct, yet interdependent concepts—*faith* and "*cumulative tradition*. A cumulative tradition represents the mundane, historical dimension of a religion, its "temples, scriptures, theological systems, dance patterns, legal and other social institutions," and so forth (156–7). Faith, conversely, resides at the personal level, "an inner experience or involvement of a particular person; the impingement on him of the transcendent, putative, or real" (156).

These two domains of religious life, Smith suggests, build on one another over time. The cumulative traditions that one inherits impact personal faith, which in turn affects the cumulative tradition. It is this interaction between faith and tradition that characterizes the basic components of religious life.

By distinguishing faith from cumulative tradition, Smith effectively redefines faith as utterly subjective and more fundamental to human life than religion. "Faith" he suggests, "is a personal quality, ... something akin to 'love'" (Smith 1962, 185). In other words, faith is a feeling, an "intangible quality" of human experience, which may not be tied to a given cumulative tradition. "There is no generic Christian faith; no 'Buddhist faith,' no 'Hindu faith,' no 'Jewish faith.' There is only my faith, and yours, and that of my Shinto friends, of my particular Jewish neighbor" (191). This repositioning is significant because it implies not only that inner faith remains separate from outward religious forms but also, more importantly, that faith is a thing accessible to any individual, even the irreligious. Everyone therefore can have faith.

In the end, Smith and Tillich helped establish faith as a way of talking about religion that could fit into the emerging pluralistic society of postwar America. Tillich described faith as ultimate concern, providing a common ground for interreligious dialogue. Smith, on the other hand, divorced faith from religious tradition, a move that allowed him to justify the comparative study of religion.

James Fowler and the Stages of Faith

The work of Tillich and Smith paved the way for future scholarship on faith as a universal dimension of human experience. In fact, their ideas directly influenced one most of the most widely discussed theories about faith to emerge during the late twentieth century: James Fowler's *Stages of Faith: The Psychology of Human Development and the Quest for Meaning*. Fowler, a professor of theology at Emory University, combined W. C. Smith's definition of faith with developmental psychology to consider how an individual's faith matures over his or her lifetime. Since its publication in 1981, *Stages of Faith*, in which he introduced the full findings from years of research, continues to be standard reading for theological education even today.

Drawing upon Smith, Fowler starts from the assumption that faith is not merely something we acquire but is innate to human beings. "I believe faith to be a human universal," he declares. "We are endowed with the nascent capacities for faith" (Fowler 1981, xiii). Even if people do not subscribe to any particular religion, they nonetheless possess the building blocks for some kind of faith that will inevitably shape how they experience the world. Faith facilitates a basic human need to find or articulate the meaning and purpose of a life. The "questions of faith," he argues, "help us to reflect on the centers of value and power that sustain our lives" (3).

Fowler also agrees with Smith's assessment that faith, although commonly linked to a religious tradition, is something altogether distinct from it. Religion represents only the outward and imperfect expression of faith, which is "at once deeper and more personal" and therefore more genuine than any observable religious tradition (9). Such a view, naturally, implies that virtually anything, not just religious traditions, could give voice to an individual's faith. It is no surprise, then, that Fowler can assert that "faith is recognizably the same phenomenon in Christians, Marxists, Hindus and Dinka, yet it is so *infinitely varied* that each person's faith is unique" [emphasis in original] (xiii). If faith is utterly personal, then anything—a religious doctrine like Trinitarian Christianity, a political philosophy such as Marxism, or the cultural traditions of the Dinka—can serve as the expression of one's particular faith.

To understand faith, Fowler advises that we must look beyond its context to examine the patterns and structures shared across all its manifestations. In pursuit of this end, he turns to the work of developmental psychologists who examined the way that individual human psychology changes from infancy to old age. Fowler observes an individual's faith as undergoing a similar process and thus identifies five (or six) stages of faith development, beginning in childhood with an intuitive stage, moving into adolescence where faith is taken as literal truth, and typically plateauing in adulthood with an appreciation for the symbolic nature of religious teachings.

At the top of this pyramid resides the handful of enlightened beings wholly immersed in their faith. He attributes this rare achievement to those shapers of history—"to Gandhi, to Martin

Luther King Jr., in the last years of his life, and to Mother Teresa of Calcutta"—who have elevated the needs of others above personal interest (Fowler 1981, 201).

Like Tillich, Fowler offers us a description of faith as utterly personal, innate to human nature, and applicable to virtually any worldview or belief system. Yet, like Smith, he aspires to give us a way of talking about faith that is inclusive of all traditions. Despite his best efforts to remain religiously neutral, however, faith development theory nonetheless privileges liberal Protestant notions of faith. First, reliance on church and scripture is relegated to the lower, adolescent stages of faith, which implicitly places Catholicism with its emphasis on hierarchy below Protestant traditions that seek an unmediated relationship between the believer and God. Likewise, fundamentalism, which embraces biblical literalism, would presumably be located below more mature stages where faith is understood as symbolic. In addition, Fowler's theory characterizes faith as a human search for the divine, which excludes some Christian perspectives that envision faith strictly as a gift from God.

The overall point here is that Fowler, following in the footsteps of W. C. Smith, Paul Tillich, and others, essentially misrepresents a particularly Western, rational, and liberal Protestant understanding of faith as a universal aspect of human nature. He overlooks and, at times, casually disregards important theological differences to impose a common structure on all worldviews. In the end, this bestows a veneer of scientific legitimacy on the notion that faith represents something for which individuals have an innate capacity and which is expressed most vividly through the diversity of all of the world's faiths, although Fowler's model implies that Protestants do it the best.

The stereotype in American popular culture

Fowler provides us with a window into how scholars subscribe to the cliché that everyone has a faith of some kind. Yet, it is important to note that scholars like Fowler only appeal to this cliché because it is already deeply ingrained in American culture more generally. Our public conversations about religion and popular culture frequently operate on the assumption that faith is simply an aspect of human nature.

Popular culture is replete with the suggestion that everyone possesses an inherent capacity for faith, and another manifestation of this cliché comes from one of my favorite science fiction franchises of all time, *Star Trek*. While known for its rather utopian version of a future human society governed by rationality and science, it does extensively explore the topic of religion. The original television series, which enjoyed a three-year run (1966–69), only dealt with religion infrequently. However, I want to suggest that in the six subsequent films featuring the original cast, faith stands front and center as a common thread connecting each installment. Specifically, the evolution of the iconic Mr. Spock, the pointed-eared Vulcan portrayed by Leonard Nimoy, illustrates the cliché that faith is an essential human quality.

For those unfamiliar with the fictional *Star Trek* universe, the series takes place in the twenty-third century, at a time when Earth is part of a larger United Federation of Planets, an intergalactic democratic consortium of species resembling the United Nations but wielding a single military known as Starfleet. Mr. Spock serves the chief science officer aboard the Starfleet vessel USS Enterprise, commanded by Captain James T. Kirk (William Shatner). Spock is the only nonhuman crew member, hailing from the planet Vulcan. Vulcan culture differs radically from human society. Vulcans value logic and reason above all else, shunning emotions as irrational and dangerous. Over the course of the series, we learn that Spock is only half Vulcan. Rejecting Vulcan tradition, Spock's father married a human woman with whom he has a child. Because Spock spends his childhood on Vulcan, however, he prefers to identify with his "logical" Vulcan nature, often taking offense at the frequent quips of his shipmates who remind him of his humanity. Throughout the three seasons of the original series, the character of Spock serves as the voice of reason, an emblem of pure logic that allows the writers to highlight the emotionalism of human beings, for better or for worse.

Over the course of the feature films, however, a different Spock unfolds, one who will learn not only to embrace his human emotions but also to appreciate the value of faith. The second film, *Star Trek*

II: The Wrath of Khan (1982), follows the crew of the Enterprise as it faces off with arch-villain Khan Noonien Sigh, a genetically modified superman bent on seeking revenge against Captain Kirk. The film's climax comes just as the warp engine of the Enterprise is about to experience a meltdown. Faced with the inevitable demise of the ship, Spock makes the snap decision to fix the engine himself, which exposes him to fatal levels of radiation. In the film's final scene, Spock, true to his Vulcan nature, explains to Kirk that logic dictated his decision. "The needs of the man," he declares, "outweigh the needs of the few."

After sacrificing himself to save the ship, Spock is literally *born again* over the course of the next film, *Star Trek III: The Search for Spock*. Picking up immediately after the previous film, the crew leaves Spock's corpse on a planet where, later, a device is tested that brings life to dead planets. Caught up in the device's aftermath, Spock's body, left for dead, is rejuvenated, and the crew rallies over the course of the film to fully restore him to life. Although one might obviously compare this rebirth to the resurrection of Christ, Spock's transformation, unlike Christ's, has only just begun.

In trying to make sense of these events, he faces an existential dilemma that will undermine his confidence in Vulcan logic, beginning a journey toward faith. It had been cold Vulcan logic that had led Spock to sacrifice himself. Faced with the imminent destruction of the Enterprise, "the needs of the many," he explained to Kirk, "outweigh the needs of the few." Yet, when Spock is reborn at the conclusion of the third film, Kirk tells Spock that his friends had risked their lives to bring him from death precisely because "the needs of the one outweigh the needs of the many." Faced with this paradox, Spock's Vulcan logic proves inadequate and he must look to his human side. Over the next three films, audiences encounter a Spock very different from the stoic and occasionally condescending creature of logic. Instead, we see an individual striving to better understand his humanity.

The pinnacle of Spock's evolution comes in the sixth and final installment of the original films, *Star Trek VI: The Undiscovered Country* (1991). The plot follows the crew of the Enterprise as they are sent on a mission to secure a peace accord between the Federation and their sworn enemies, the Klingon Empire. While en route, Valeris (Kim Catrall), a young Vulcan lieutenant set to replace Spock as chief science officer on the Enterprise, privately confesses her anxiety over the mission to Spock:

Valeris: Sir, I address you as a kindred intellect. Do you not recognize that a turning point has been reached in the affairs of the Federation?

Spock: History is replete with turning points, Lieutenant. You must have faith.

Valeris: Faith?

Spock: That the universe will unfold as it should.

Valeris: But is this logical? Surely we must.

Spock: Logic? Logic is the beginning of wisdom, Valeris, not the end.

Spock passes the torch to his young successor, signifying the completion of his journey, not only as a Starfleet officer but also, more importantly, because his quest for wisdom, which began in logic, has found its natural end in faith. In this exchange, we can see our cliché at work. Spock's search for his own humanity leads him to faith; it is faith that makes one distinctively human, and it is this realization—to be human is to have faith—to which all of us must aspire. Spock, now the esteemed Federation ambassador of galactic peace, has achieved the final stage of Fowler's model: Universalizing Faith. Only as he embraces that which makes him essentially human—an innate capacity for faith—can Spock realize the wisdom that has eluded his Vulcan commitment to reason.

Conclusion: The power of cliché in everyday life

Popular culture always tells us a great deal about our own norms and expectations. They provide the scripts through which we act out our public and private lives. These cases illustrate the power that resides in the assertion that everyone has a faith. In American society today, to declare one's faith is to claim something about one's essential humanity. Thus, when someone insists that everyone has a faith of some kind, they tell us less about faith itself than they reveal about their own motivations. It represents an attempt to impose an arbitrary framework around an otherwise unconnected set of beliefs and experiences about the world, one that elevates faith above all else. Yet, throughout this chapter, we have witnessed how these attempts to valorize faith as an essential human quality rest not on objective observations of human behavior but on ideology. If we depict religion or faith as human nature, we inadvertently render alternative viewpoints as misguided. Atheists become misguided fools who simply fail to realize that they have a faith. Moreover, it obscures the very real distinctions between different systems of belief and ways of knowing. Science appears as simply another form of faith, despite the fact that, unlike Protestant belief, scientific claims are always open to scrutiny and falsification.

Claiming that everyone has a faith reduces all points of view to private matters but simultaneously masks the way that Western Protestant modes of thought continue to dictate the terms by which we make sense of the world. Though it appears neutral, this cliché is, as Bruce Lincoln suggests, a myth, ideology in narrative form, that carries forth a particular agenda. In effect, it informs us that religion is everywhere, faith is our alpha and omega, our beginning and our end as human beings, and it (particularly its Protestant variation) is good. While we cannot do without clichés, it behooves us to think critically about their inherent power to shape the world we all must inhabit.

10

"Religion is bullshit"

Rebekka King

Perhaps you've seen him so many times before that he has become a caricature, a trope, in the realm of religious studies classrooms. His eyes are ever eager to roll to the back of his head at the mention of religious devotion, superhuman beings, or miraculous events. He enters the room with an ornery swagger; he's well versed in arguments garnered from the likes of Christopher Hitches, Sam Harris, and Bill Maher. If this class is not required, then his *raison d'être* is clear: he's here to argue (a performance of polemics) and to gain ammunition (apologetics) in support of his foundational belief concerning religion, religious adherents, and religious worlds—it is all, more or less, bullshit.

Your reaction to his dismissive statement will depend on your own relationship to the subject matter of studying religion. Perhaps, like me, you see a former version of yourself in him? Do the evocative words of Bob Dylan—"I was so much older then: I'm younger than that now"—echo in your assessment of his motivations? He will come around, you think. He will discover, as you did, that the study of religion is not about right or wrong or about things that are real and things that are imaginary. Instead, ours is a task dedicated to questions of social consequences, distribution of power, or as I tell my own students almost daily, "what the 'doing,' does." On the opposite end of the spectrum, perhaps you recoil? "Religion is everything," you think to yourself.

After all, even Karl Marx, when pointing out that religion was the "opium of the masses," equates it with "the sigh of the oppressed" and "the heart of a heartless world." Your task in this case becomes one in which you seek to correct his perspective, to uncover the myriad ways that religions themselves serve as inspirations for human flourishing. After all, you think, people are generally good. While problems may at times emerge, such is the cost of social interactions. When we think of religion, we might think to ourselves, we should shift our focus to the positive outcomes that accompany instances where groups organize around supposedly universal and altruistic concepts, like love, justice, and fidelity (see, for instance, Jennifer Eyl's chapter on how "Religion makes people moral" in this volume).

In either case, your mission, as you see it, is clear. Mr. Bullshit has arrived in this class with a perfunctory theory of religion and you—armed with a more nuanced perspective and informed by some of the greatest minds in the discipline of religious studies, including your professor and the authors of the preceding chapters in this volume—must begin the process of uncoiling his misperceptions. While I would like to wish you good speed, suggest that you need not read this final chapter, and instead begin in haste your rebuttal, I cannot. Instead, I offer a warning: your own simplistic assessment and desire to correct, in and of itself, is bullshit.

Social contexts: Bullshiters and bullshitees

Take a closer look: "bullshit" is both a noun and a verb. There is a difference between the production of bullshit and the recognition of it. First, it is an act of classification. American philosopher Harry Frankfurt famously published a brief and amusing reflection on the nature of bullshit in common parlance that proffers a philosophical analysis of what it is. In his work, *On Bullshit* (2005), Frankfurt differentiates bullshit from lying by indicating a higher level of deceit and often (but not always) an accompanying sense of pretentiousness. A liar who knows that she is lying remains committed to an idea of truth, whereas the bullshiter lacks any hint of veracity and instead is committed solely to the aesthetics of her lie and what she might gain from it. In other words, she is trying to get away with something, is being intentionally insincere, and does not value the intelligence of her audience. The power of this insincerity rests in the ways that she intermixes truth and lies as unlikely bedfellows. Frankfurt explains that the bullshiter is "neither on the side of the true nor on the side of the false. His eye is not on the facts at all, as the eyes of the honest man and of the liar are, except insofar as they may be pertinent to his interest in getting away with what he says" (Frankfurt 2005, 56). Frankfurt provides convincing evidence for bullshit as a category of analysis and differentiates it from other terms such as humbug, bluffing, and hot air (cf. Peters 2015). His focus is on the bullshiter and how she deploys bullshit. Frankfurt offers little by way of a discussion of what bullshit does in its social contexts, nor does he address the question of what the act of calling something bullshit might do. Under what circumstances does one become the bullshitee (i.e., the person who recognizes it in others), with what cultural assumptions, what categories analysis, and what social currency?

The notion that "religion is bullshit" is bound up with the cultural context of late modern societies' various renditions of the self as individual, self-directed, and discerning (see Martin 2014, McCutcheon 2003, Taylor 1989). Something becomes bullshit only when it is recognized as such. In the previous scenario, religion is just religion until it is declared to be bullshit. The student who makes this declaration is able to do so because he is confident in his own abilities to evaluate the various beliefs, practices, institutions, and so forth that are contained under the banner of religion. His confidence in his capacity to do so depends on the idea that, as members of democratic civil societies, we should each assume the role of informed citizens capable of accurately forming opinions about events and activities in the world. Related to this assumption is that idea that not only can we recognize bullshit but also we can (and perhaps should) do something about it.

In this way, labeling something as bullshit is an act of rejection. Bullshit is undesirable—it is a distraction from the true state of affairs and therefore must be sussed out and eliminated. For those who ascribe to the "religion is bullshit" maxim, religion somehow serves as an obstacle between individuals and reality. Their data is drawn from a number of sources including personal experiences, the witticisms of Jon Stewart (discussed later in this chapter), and trends that continue to resonate in the aftermath of the height of New Atheism, alongside a long history of larger projects of counter discourses concerning religion (e.g., see Modern 2011, Smith 2003, Young 2015; cf. Warner 2002) and the modern project whereby religion is demarcated as a separate category by the general public as well as scholars who study it (see Asad 1993, Fitzgerald 2000, Masuzawa 2005, McCutcheon 1997).

As a rhetorical practice, the declarative statement, "religion (or any other social phenomenon) is bullshit," reveals very little about the content of religion but instead compels a consideration of the individual(s) employing said statement and its performative potentiality. In other words, it likely tells us nothing about religion, but it does reveal something about the statement's utterer—the bullshitee, that is, the apparent recipient of bullshit—and his or her social context. With this in mind, I want to think about what bullshit does as a rhetorical practice, rather than what it tells us about religion (which, as I have already said, is very little).

In the statement, "religion is bullshit," I see three related yet distinct modalities at work: skepticism, dissent or disdain, and despair (there are most certainly others, but these are the three that I find most interesting). Each serves as a critical cultural marker in contemporary North American society and each adopts a specific position vis-à-vis religion. There is an underlying ethic at work for our bullshitee that frames religion along a spectrum of either (1) things that are false, (2) things that are wrong, or (3) things that are deplorable. As such, we see religion constituted as some combination of imaginary beliefs, insolent practices, and the unjust distribution of power and authority. In what follows, I will explore these three modalities by placing them in their historical context and drawing on contemporary and popular examples of their execution. In doing so, I want to remind you (as I'm sure your professor already has made clear) that ours is an attempt to think about the ways that people frame the world, not to make evaluative statements regarding religion. We're not interested in whether or not the bullshitee is right or wrong in his assessment, instead we're looking for the causes behind it.

Modality one—skepticism: Religion is bullshit because it is "false"

In its contemporary form, skepticism toward religion as manifested by groups such as the New Atheists takes the form of rejecting religious beliefs and behaviors seen to be tied to the existence and commands of supernatural, non-empirical beings (see Amarasingam 2010, Beattie 2008, Hulsether 2008). In this context, our bullshitee's claim is really about the lack of evidence concerning the likelihood of supernatural beings and the practices that surround them. As a historical project, skepticism finds its roots in thinkers like Hume, Hobbes, Freud, Marx, Nietzsche, and Darwin and in the onset of the scientific method. Religion is perceived to be bullshit because it makes claims that are not empirically verifiable by modern science: we "know," for example, that virgins do not give birth, men cannot survive for years on one grain of rice a day, and the sun does not unexpectedly halt its circumambulation of the earth.

Historically speaking, most scholars did not use the term "bullshit" in reference to religion—such vulgarities would not befit Victorian ears—but we can locate among the aforementioned scholars a similar attitude or approach to religion. Early theorists of religion such as anthropologists Edward Tylor (1832–1917) and James Frazer (1854–1931) proposed that religion emerged in "primitive societies" as a means of providing explanations for mysterious occurrences in an era before science. Tylor, for example, theorized that the origins of religions rest in animism, the notion that all natural phenomena are or can be possessed by a soul or spirit. In Tylor's view, animism developed into more complex beliefs about divine powers and beings and ultimately culminated in the conceptualization of a "high god" and the development of monotheism. In his assessment, religion's persistence in the modern world can be accounted for through a theory of "survivals" (i.e., traditions and customs that carry on in a particular culture even after they no longer serve their initial purpose). In a similar vein, Frazer saw religion as originating in magic and attempts on the part of early societies to influence the natural world. He saw religion as a later and, in some ways, less sophisticated development—whereas magic seeks to directly influence the world, religion relies on the intervention of spirits or gods. His famous work, *The Golden Bough* (published in several volumes and editions from 1890–1915), offers a comparison between different religious myths and concludes with the suggestion that science will ultimately replace religion as part of a larger project to understand the world and organize our knowledge of it.

But how do we know what we know? Cultural theorist Bruno Latour argues that the taken-for-granted approach we have in regard to scientific findings is a rather recent development. The introduction of the scientific method initiated a novel way of thinking about what counts as "fact" or "evidence." Rather than relying on pure mathematics or physics, early proponents of the scientific method promoted experimentation as the pinnacle of scientific discovery. One in which evidence was deemed factual in so far as an experiment could be replicated by credible witnesses in uncontaminated laboratories (Latour 1993). You likely have been socialized into this process of observation, hypothesis, testing, and theory as you learned the scientific method in school.

While the assumptions we make about gathering knowledge from science all seems very straightforward, it has several related consequences. Specialized knowledge and training are required to ensure that those so-called credible witnesses are equipped to undertake, replicate, and evaluate experiments and to accurately report their findings. Science, alongside education, medicine, and the judicial process, was increasingly differentiated into a separate realm with a hierarchy of experts whose authority lies in the idea that experiments could be performed in such a way that they were neutral—free of outside political, religious, or social influences.[1] The assumptions made about the possible objectivity of the scientific method reinforced the notion that we might begin to conceptualize the world according to facts, hypotheses, and falsehoods, with an aim toward increasing the first and diminishing the third. Such attention to empirical evidence enabled a shift in thinking that links truth and observation. Hypotheses—those things about which we cannot be absolutely certain—were left to sit in the middle space waiting to be eventually categorized as either fact or falsehood.

It is here that "belief" enters the realm of engagement. In this era we see a shift from belief as indicating social affiliation to belief as indicating cognitive assent (see Smith 1977, 1979; see also Lopez 1998 and Sean McCloud's chapter, "Religions are belief systems," in this volume).[2] Belief moves from something that one "does" to something that one "has"—it becomes tangible, an object available for examination and subject to all of the same empirical procedures we have available to us in the scientific method. As something that we seek to empirically verify but are not always able to, belief occupies that sinewy space between fact and falsehood. In other words, belief is likened to a hypothesis (we often hear religious people speak about "taking a leap of faith" or "believing against all odds"). Belief becomes a battleground between conviction and skepticism and in many instances a litmus test for religious affiliation and/or lack thereof. Those who do not believe do so because for them the evidence is not there.

Lest you think that skepticism rests in a religionless realm of science, empiricism, and rational thought, it should be noted that the longer history of skepticism and nonbelief is one that is tied to religious affiliation and devotion (Smith 2003; see also Hatch 1989). It stems as much from the attempts on the part of religious adherents to find common ground between religion, science, and history. As historian James Turner famously notes, "If anyone is to be arraigned for deicide [that is, killing God], it is not Charles Darwin but his adversary Bishop Samuel Wilberforce, not the godless Robert Ingersoll but the Godly Beecher family" (Turner 1985, xiii). In other words, it is not so much Darwin's evolutionary theory nor Ingersoll's promotion of freethinking and agnosticism that served as an impulse for skepticism. Instead, the source is closer to home, in figures such as the Church of England cleric, Wilberforce, who worked to end slavery in the British Empire, or the evangelical Beecher family, who advocated for civil rights and social reforms. With this in mind, we can begin to think about the ways that bullshit might serve as part of a larger insider discourse in which religious adherents attempt to make sense of the competing truth claims between science and their own religious traditions and, in at least some cases, choose science over and against religion.

In his sociological study of Muslim apostates (i.e., people who left the religion), Simon Cottee (2015) notes that skepticism often stems from a deep religiosity. Cottee interviews former Muslims from the United Kingdom and Canada to determine what factors contributed to their departure from Islam. He discovers that those who are stricken by doubts are often those who were most actively engaged in intellectual reflection, traditional piety, and a close examination of scripture. For many of the former Muslims who Cottee interviewed, their rejection of Islam was linked to their inability to bring the Qur'an in line with their understanding of history and/or science. As one of his subjects, Omar reports, traditional teachings about the existence of God, predestination, and the divine creation of the world served as lynchpins for his increased doubt. Eventually, he demarks it as bullshit: "The problem I had was when I started doubting the existence of God. What if this is just bullshit, what if it's just nonsense?" (Cottee 2015, 33). In this context, Omar ultimately determines that the existence of God is inconsistent with his understanding of how the universe operates and as such must be rejected.

Likewise, controversial Episcopal bishop John Shelby Spong calls for a reconsideration of those Christian teachings that are not clearly aligned with scientific findings. Spong does not reject his religion outright; instead he seeks to remove those elements that contradict science. In a lecture Spong gave at the Chautauqua Institute in upstate New York, he recalls a conversation he had with astronomer Carl Sagan concerning this very idea. As Spong tells it, Sagan ran up to him at a conference shaking with excitement and posed the question as to what the ascension of Jesus would look like from the perspective of astrophysics. "Did you know that if Jesus literally ascended into the sky and if he travelled at the speed of light one hundred and eighty-six miles per second give or take a mile or two, that he hasn't yet escaped our galaxy?" Sagan may have been telling a joke, but for Spong, the story points to an understanding of religion that needs to evolve beyond those elements that he sees as failing to stand up against empiricism.[3]

While Spong retains his religious affiliation, choosing instead to alter Christianity by removing those miraculous and non-empirical elements, Omar (and others featured in Cottee's book) ultimately finds he cannot retain his religious affiliation, thus becoming an apostate. In each of these cases we have an evaluation of the tradition vis-à-vis its scriptural or doctrinal claims that are brought into conversation with scientific facts. Here, the assumption is that the authors of religious scriptures may have misunderstood reality, but we know better. What is interesting is the assumption that we know better, because we know empirically. In this way beliefs and knowledge can be realigned to reflect what we can actually observe.

That being said, there is usually more to the story than empiricism at work in the declaration that "religion is bullshit." For example, our bullshitee might say that believing in faeries is silly or implausible but is unlikely to categorize it as bullshit. For the most part, the belief in faeries has limited effects on our daily lives or how we interact with others. Belief is often tied to value judgments and ethical considerations (as in instances in which one might or might not believe in evolution, the death penalty, or access to reproductive technologies). Thus while skepticism, the suspicion that religion is bullshit because it is false, might serve as a starting point for our consideration of what the declaration does for the bullshitee, there are larger social concerns at play. The bullshitee who is taking a skeptical approach is organizing information along a framework that sees observation as the first order of knowledge (how we know what we know) but consideration is needed of the ethical consequences of knowledge (why what we know matters).

Modality two – dissent and disdain: Religion is bullshit because it is "morally wrong"

While both Tylor and Frazer saw religion as an understandable, "primitive" error, rendered as bullshit in so far as it was false, other scholars were more explicit in their critique of religion's origins. For example, Sigmund Freud (1856–1939) saw religion as derived from a collective neurosis whereby the gods emerged as a reflection of the parent-child relationship. This theory, which is conversant with Freud's Oedipus complex, suggests that the gods serve as a substitute for, or an attempt to return to, the safety of the infantile state and the security of the womb. Religion in this context was something that needed to be overcome to liberate humans from this childhood fixation. In *Totem and Taboo* (1913), Freud writes, "It is not to be supposed that men were inspired to create their first system of the universe by purely speculative curiosity. The practical need for controlling the world around them must have played its part" (Freud 1950, 78). In this way, Freud saw at work in the origins of religion more than just a mistake but rather an inner illusion that needs to be overcome and defeated for the betterment of society, although Freud was hesitant to say that he thought people were capable of doing so (Freud 1989).

In the final episode of his immensely popular late night show, Jon Stewart dedicated his concluding rant to the varieties of bullshit we see at work in contemporary culture.[4] Stewart, along with other comedians who adopt this genre, is known for delineating the absurdities of American political processes and generating popular indignation through humor (see Clark and Dierberg 2012 and Lindvall 2015). Stewart identifies different typologies of bullshit, noting that almost everything we encounter in life is in some way infused with it. While it is often found in the realm of "every day, organic, free-range bullshit," such as the innocuous description of a homely baby's cuteness offered as a social grace, there also exists a more nefarious form of bullshit that Stewart identifies as institutionalized bullshit, generated by the "Bullshitocracy." This term refers to an elite group responsible for the creation of bullshit—policies, practices, and products—designed to confuse ordinary people and to distract them from what is really going on. True to form, Stewart layers his examples, interspersing the political with the comical, and concludes by directing his audience that "the best defense against bullshit is vigilance; if you smell something say something."

Under this guise, detecting bullshit is aligned with common sense, and its denotation is a moral act in opposition to malevolent forces. To call something "bullshit" is not necessarily to question its existence (as in the case of our first modality) but rather to question its worth. It is to regard it with disdain and see it as something we must oppose for the betterment of society. While not exclusively an American ideal, there is something at the core of American identity that engenders dissent (Young 2015). Active opposition to bullshit is the duty of every citizen—from the revolutionary impulse of Alexander Hamilton to the early feminism of Susan B. Anthony, from the counterculture critiques of Timothy Leary to the call to action of Martin Luther King Jr.—and in its contemporary renditions of right-to-life and #blacklivesmatter activists, we see bullshit as a rallying cry and an expression of dissent from or disagreement with the larger social structures at work that contribute to the moral fabric of society.

Calling something bullshit, however, might take a less political and more personal tone and render itself as disdain.[5] In this context, the declaration that religion is bullshit serves as an ethical or a moral critique. We need only to turn to public faces of religion to find a plethora of examples that provide opportunities for a critique casting religious adherents and their supporters as bullshiters. When I googled "religion is bullshit," one of the first items that came up was a website discussing the Duggar family and their reality television show, *19 Kids and Counting* (TLC). The show, which began as *17 Kids and Counting,* aired for ten seasons and purported to present to Americans wholesome small-town, midwestern virtues infused with conservative Christian values. The Duggars are vocal opponents of birth control, LGBTQI+ rights, and sex outside of marriage. Instead they promote a patriarchal and heteronormative family structure that favors homeschooling and the restriction of their children's names to those beginning with a single consonant.[6] As devoted Baptists, the Duggar family focused their energies on godly obedience, sexual purity, and moral rectitude. Theirs was the image of a perfect, all-American family, but one that was revealed to be a façade through a series of highly publicized events in the spring of 2015. While the family framed its public face as one of sexual purity and domestic harmony, a police report surfaced alleging multiple sexual assaults of five underage girls by the Duggars' oldest son Josh. While the family had been aware of the assaults, which included four of Josh Duggar's younger sisters, they concealed them from the public eye. Revelations concerning Josh Duggar continued to flare up in the ensuing months when in August 2015 his name was included on the list of Ashley Madison clients (a dating website that caters to married men looking to arrange extramarital relationships) and again in November 2015 when he was accused of sexual assault at a strip club (charges that later proved to be fabricated, although Duggar's presence at the strip club was not).

The Duggars are low-hanging fruit when it comes to identifying bullshit in regard to religious adherents, and many of their critics used that very language to describe them. Certainly the allegations of sexual assault are distressing in multiple ways, but what brings the Duggar family into the realm of bullshit is their excessive criticism of the very sexual activities it turns out their eldest (read: favorite) son engaged in. It is a classic case of "do as I say, not as I do." The lack of consistency between words and actions calls to mind larger ethical assumptions about the currency of sincerity and our ability to evaluate it in others (see Keane 2002). We assume that there exists some sort of hierarchy between thoughts and words whereby what we say reveals something about who we are as ethical agents. Those who would declare the Duggar family's religiosity to be bullshit do so not because of something empirical, but because of something ethical. Even more pressing in the eyes of their critics, the Duggar example is cause for concern because they reaped social and financial benefits from their deployment of their particular variety of bullshit.

Modality three – despair: Religion is bullshit because it is "terrible"

In the farming community in which I grew up, it was not uncommon to see homemade written signs along backcountry roads advertising "Bulls for Rent." While these signs are increasingly rare today, my memory of them prompted me to investigate the point origins for bullshit—the bull itself. Along with the idea that there is power in declaring that something is bullshit, there is something significant in the term itself and what bulls signify. Why do we say bullshit and not dog shit, or bird shit, or even cow shit? To paraphrase Jonathan Z. Smith, what difference does this difference make (Smith 2004)?

So it was that I found myself on the dairy farm of one of my childhood friends. "We don't keep bulls here," she explained to me, noting that it's not safe to have such aggressive animals around her young children. I nod and make a superficial reference to Spanish matadors and red flags, which falls flat as my friend walks me through the specifics of bovine breeding practices. Bulls, of course, should be differentiated from steers, which are commonplace on the farm—both are male cattle but steers are castrated and, as my friend pointed out, "taste great on the BBQ." That is, they produce a leaner and cleaner tasting meat. Unlike cows, which produce milk, a bull's usefulness lies in its reproductive capacities. While my memory of people renting out bulls for the purpose of breeding is accurate, the practice is less common now than when I was a child. Artificial insemination is preferable because it allows for a controlled environment and the same source can be used more than once. Farmers will sometimes borrow or rent bulls for breeding but only as an alternative measure when artificial insemination fails or there is a need to "clean up" the herd. In this case, the bull is kept on the farm for a period of time so that it is provided the opportunity to copulate with all of the cows. With a live bull, it is not advisable to reuse the same bull for fear of inbreeding. My friend laughed as I described my interest in bulls. "They're generally seen as stinky, dumb animals," she said shrugging her shoulders. "They only have two purposes—breeding and dinner." I pressed on and asked whether there is a discernible difference between bull shit and cow shit? She laughed and rolled her eyes, "Shit is shit," she retorted.

While my friend sees the utility of bulls as limited, I cannot help but see significance in the fact that the bull is something that is feared and restricted to certain times and places. My last question was perhaps naïve, but my time on the farm suggests that the bull and its shit are revealing because of their elusiveness. The bull is a hostile and aggressive beast that charges wildly at waving flags and children and must be contained, only to be used when needed; its meat is less desirable and as such it is castrated; it is an essential resource but one that, when overused, causes damage to the future fertility of the herd; and it is quickly being removed from farm life. Instead, its semen is packaged, commodified, and employed at an opportune time so as to avoid the uncertainty that accompanies natural copulation. What is revealed is that the bull itself is a rarity on the farm because the risks associated with keeping it around are too high. The restriction or absence of bulls, of course, means that their manure would likewise be uncommon. Bullshit it appears is not as ubiquitous in the spaces in which we might expect it.

It is with this image of bullshit that is expected but not evident which I close. Jon Stewart's call that we identify and name bullshit only works so far as we are able to recognize it. If we assume that "shit is shit," we run the risk of equating the specific with the general, the sensational with the serious, and evidence with expectations. Ours is a culture focused on the means through which we represent and denote the self in social settings. In the preceding two examples, the common point of origins referred to a certain assumption about an individual's capacity to weigh evidence and to infer the ethical consequences of statements. The skeptical modality evokes the notion that religion is bullshit because it conflicts with how we understand the world to be, and the modality of dissent and disdain reveals that it is bullshit because its adherents do not practice what they preach. Both of these points presume a certain degree of cultural capital, specialized knowledge, and our own capacities to locate the cause of a lie. But what about those instances in which the source eludes us? We see the shit and look for the bull but it simply isn't there, or at least not in the form we expect.

A third facet of bullshit remains that speaks to what I see as an almost visceral component of bullshit: those moments where nothing seems to make sense, or put more bluntly, when "shit hits the fan." In these instances, bullshit is not clever or calculated but rather derives from chaos and despair, and we're just not sure where it came from. In a political era that has been increasingly defined by its widening gap between those who possess power and those who lack it, to identify bullshit provides a temporary escape or release from the social conditions in which we find ourselves but fails to make a difference therein. Think, for example, of a single mother denied promotion at work, a young black man who is pulled over for DWB (i.e., "driving while black"), or countless other injustices that stem from social forces that gain momentum from their ambiguity and seemingly unknown sources. In the face of such an obvious imbalance of power, the declaration, "this is bullshit," provides some therapeutic relief in the moment of its uttering.

This form of bullshit is different in degree but not in kind. For Marx, as with Freud, religion is an illusion, but it is not religion that needs to be cast aside. Religion is secondary to a larger system of economic and political exploitation that needs to be defeated. Marx and his co-writer, Engels, argue that religion can take two forms: first, as an ideological tool employed by the ruling class and, second, as has already been alluded to, as a place to redirect one's frustrations and experiences of suffering (Marx 1970). When Marx observes that religion is the sigh of the oppressed, we see religion doing something very similar to what the expression, "this is bullshit," does for our bullshitee. In the context of an experience in which it appears that whoever is to blame is invisible and inaccessible, bullshit, regardless of whether or not you can smell it, is at least something that can be named.

For these reasons, I suggest you take a closer look at the source. Not of the bullshit itself—there is no need for you to follow my lead and attempt to track down a farmer, a bull, or excrement—but of those who name it and force us to contend with it; pay close attention to the places where it appears to be absent. The imagined student from the beginning of this chapter may very well be conflicted, crazy, or both, but he may also be on to something. His equation of religion and bullshit, it seems, is at the very heart of our social order and our conceptions of the self. These components are necessary to us as we begin the process of delineating an academic study of religion as a social and discursive entity. It is not about whether or not his reading of religion is right or wrong but where it comes from and what it does. With this in mind, I suggest that rather than silencing or dismissing the bullshitee in your class, you ask some follow-up questions. Does he think religion is bullshit because it contains teachings that depart from a scientific understanding of the world? Is he concerned about perceived moral inconsistencies on the part of religious adherents? Or is he articulating something larger—a dissatisfaction that is not easily named or identified? It is from this starting point that you undertake the task of studying religion. Your professor has given you the data and the theories with which to begin to understand religion and to move beyond the different clichés outlined in this volume, but your professor can only take you so far. It is up to you to do the hard work of analysis and critique and to interrogate the evidence before you. At the end of the day it doesn't matter whether or not religion is bullshit—the term is an empty signifier. What matters is your ability to weigh evidence, locate sources, and pay critical attention to both your scholarly process and product. You may find yourself mired in shit but at least you'll be in good company.

Notes

Chapter 2

1 See Maher, 2014b.

2 See Maher, 2014a.

3 This trend is alive and well today as most introductory textbooks in religious studies still follow the world religions paradigm (WRP), which is a methodological approach that compares presumed similarities between approximately eight to ten "religions" based primarily on a selection of scriptural passages and what has been popularized by certain figures such as Martin Luther and Gandhi.

4 It should be noted that this claim is also a cliché since it reduces people's behavior to their religious identity.

5 This position, while now retracted, offers a striking example of the idea of social evolution, in which the "Christian West" is perceived to be at a higher level of social development because of its embrace of liberalism, secularism, and capitalism. See Hirsi Ali 2015a.

Chapter 3

1 In a sense, Augustine is talking about religion more broadly, since he considers Catholic Christianity the only legitimate religion.

2 The work of Frans de Waal 2006, Marco Iacoboni 2009, and Benjamin James Fraser 2010 provide helpful reading on this question. See also, Katz 2000, Gallese 2001, Brosnan et al. 2005, Joyce 2006, Warneken and Tomasello 2006.

3 The Prosocial Choice Test explores altruism between pairs of chimpanzees held in separate rooms while remaining visible and audible to one another. The test presents chimps with green and red tokens that they hand over to a human tester. If the chimp chooses red, she is rewarded with food; if she chooses green, both she and her partner chimp are rewarded with food. De Waal's study demonstrates that chimps will disproportionately choose the altruistic color so they and their partners can receive food. The test requires a partner, of course, and when a partner is absent, the chimps randomly select red and green. Curiously, when a chimp pressures its partner to choose the green token (by banging, screaming, and spitting

water), the partner often refuses and instead chooses the red token. See de Waal 2013, esp. 117–23.

4 It goes without saying that humans do not always act prosocially, nor do we consistently feel empathy toward others. While Iacoboni's research examines the reflex of feeling the pain of others in mirror neurons, his research does not examine how we socially construct categories of "us" and "other," thereby concluding that the pain of others is meaningless. For a meaningful and contemporary meditation on the human reaction to the suffering of others, see Sontag 2003.

5 De Waal's research challenges the notion that humans are innately selfish, brutish, and inclined toward social Darwinism. He critiques what he calls the "Veneer Theory" of morality—that if one scratches the surface of a regular, decent person, one finds a barbaric and selfish inner core that is kept at bay by social customs, moral proscriptions, religion, and legal codes.

6 For example, in 2013, the US Army finished removing biblical citations from the scopes of its high-powered rifles. The scopes had been stamped with John 8:12 and 2 Corinthians 4:6 (i.e., JN8:12 and 2COR4:6) for strengthening and protecting troops during the wars in Iraq and Afghanistan (see Editor 2010, 130). While the removal offer was announced in 2010, it was not complete until 2013.

7 According to Public Religion Research Institute's Robert Jones, "As Americans tune in to the Super Bowl this year, fully half of fans—as many as 70 million Americans—believe there may be a twelfth man on the field influencing the outcome. Significant numbers of American sports fans believe in invoking assistance from God on behalf of their favorite team or believe the divine may be playing out its own purpose in the game" (Kaleem 2014).

8 Whitehouse is at the forefront of an approach to the study of religion called Cognitive Science of Religion (CSR), which has a growing number of proponents and detractors. For a strong critique of CSR, see Arnal and McCutcheon 2013, esp. the chapter titled "Will Your Cognitive Anchor Hold in the Storms of Culture?"

9 Whitehouse names this "why-type" mode the *doctrinal mode* (see Whitehouse 2004, 87–104). To be clear, it does not take the doctrinal mode of religiosity to tell us that "thou shall not steal" or "thou shall not murder." Such tenets do not, in fact, have anything to do with religion per se; they have to do with prosociality. In no stable, sustainable human society has it ever been acceptable to randomly murder, steal, lie, cheat, etc. These behaviors are typically unacceptable although their definitions may change (i.e., "murder" to one group of people may be called "state sponsored execution" or "justified war" to others).

10 As Andrew Stephen puts it, "Americans truly believe in the manifest destiny of their country. 'In God We Trust', it says on their coins: they think they have God's automatic imprimatur" (Stephen 2002, 13).

11 The Panopticon, originally designed by Jeremy Bentham, is a plan for incarceration that allows one single guard to have visual access to all inmate cells simultaneously. The structure is circular in shape and all cells face the center, with a guard station in the middle, facing out toward the cells. Thus, the structure allows for surveillance of all cells at once. Naturally, one guard cannot watch all cells simultaneously, but the Panopticon works because inmates cannot tell if they are being watched or not. Because one *could* be watched, and perhaps *is* being watched, inmates are more likely to police their own behavior. Michel Foucault observes that via the Panopticon, "the perfection of power should tend to render its actual exercise unnecessary; that this architectural apparatus should be a machine for creating and sustaining a power relation independent of the person who exercises it" (Foucault 1995, 201).

12 As Norenzayan observes, "Make your first move a cooperative one, then do unto others what others do unto you, and you will go far in your social life" (2013, 5).

13 Laura Pinto and Selena Nemorin write, "The Elf on the Shelf essentially teaches the child to accept an external form of non-familial surveillance in the home when the elf becomes the source of power and judgment, based on a set of rules attributable to Santa Claus... By inviting The Elf on the Shelf simultaneously into their play-world and real lives, children are taught to accept or even seek out external observation of their actions outside of their caregivers and familial structures. Broadly speaking, The Elf on the Shelf serves functions that are aligned to the official functions of the Panopticon. In doing so, it contributes to the shaping of children as governable subjects." See Pinto and Nemorin 2014.

14 This notion is captured even in ancient sources. The fifth century BCE "Sisyphus Fragment" (of contested authorship) argues that gods were invented by humans to frighten wicked men into behaving well. I thank Erin Roberts (in an unpublished paper) for her notion of "children's gods" (e.g., Santa Claus, the Tooth Fairy, Easter Bunny, Jack Frost, etc.), as primers for bigger, adult gods.

Chapter 4

1 Eliade was not entirely consistent in this message, although it was the primary way that he described the function of the sacred. For instance, one such inconsistency can be found in Eliade's description of the label "sacred" as a choice that humans make in describing certain phenomena, rather than a force that cannot be controlled and that superimposes itself on humans. See Eliade 1996, 13ff.

2 See the Web site for Gobind Sadan (www.gobindsadan.org); Fisher's role with the organization is detailed there but is also briefly mentioned in her book blurbs on Amazon.com (for instance, see www.amazon.com/Living-Religions-9th-Mary-Fisher/dp/0205956408/ref=sr_1_1?ie=UTF8&qid=1467913494&sr=8-1&keywords=mary+pat+fisher).

3 Capitalization of this term is used consistently by Alcoholics Anonymous, which further proves the larger point of this essay.

Chapter 5

1 On the topic of Abraham Lincoln, religion, and historical problems with the extant source material, see Mansfield 2012. Some scholars suggest that the religious rhetoric in Lincoln's political speeches demonstrates that he was 'politically religious,' although the concept of "political religion" is only passingly defined. Allen C. Guelzo, for example, refers to Lincoln as "one of the most determined and eloquent apostles of liberal capitalism" (Guelzo 2003, 18). Glen E. Thurow tautologically argues that "Lincoln's religion, as we know it, is part of his political rhetoric and cannot be divorced from it" (Thurow 1976). For a critique of the category of "political religion," see Stowers (2007).

   Of note, some scholars include Thomas Jefferson and Andrew Johnson with Lincoln as US presidents who were not explicitly "religious." Thomas Jefferson was raised an Anglican and, as revealed in his (fairly extensive) extant correspondence, was later a deist. Johnson was known to attend Methodist services with his wife and, occasionally, Catholic mass. When asked about his practice, Johnson maintained that he supported "the doctrine of the Bible, as taught and practiced by Jesus Christ" (quoted in Milton 1930, 80).

2 I discovered late in the process of writing this piece that Burton Mack briefly references Kennedy's speech in his introduction to *Myth and the Christian Nation: A Social Theory of Religion* (Mack 2008, 2–3).

3 Transcript of Kennedy's speech accessed via National Public Radio (NPR) archives. "Transcript: JFK's Speech on His Religion," December 5, 2007. Available at http://www.npr.org/templates/story/story.php?storyId=16920600.

4 In this passage, Arnal and McCutcheon are reflecting on the works of Talal Asad, William T. Cavanaugh, and Slavoj Žižek.

5 Take, for example, Sandra Byrd, *The One Year Be-Tween You and God: Devotions for Girls* (2012) or Jenny B. Jones, *Just Between You and Me: A Novel of Losing Fear and Finding God* (2009). The so-called Biblezine genre (an amalgamation of New Testament texts and pop culture magazine dating and fashion advice) also evokes similar themes throughout. See *Revolve: The Complete New Testament* (2003) and *Real: The Complete New Testament* (2005).

6 Rihanna's comment was picked up by popular media sites like *Huffington Post* and numerous religiously themed Web sites, which debated its implications, given the sometimes racy themes in Rihanna's music. See, for example, "Rihanna Talks Relationship with God" (Thomasos 2013).

7 For more on the concept of "belief" in Buddhism, see Lopez 1998 and Schilbrack 2014, esp. 55–81.

8 Moreover, the ancients also did not hold "public" and "private" as hard and fast categories; households were sites of social dealings such as business deals or communal meals, thus the religiously coded practices that took place within the walls of a home were not excluded from the civic sphere. Scholarship on this issue is still evolving, with increasing recognition that the categories of public/private are problematic. Not only are they not fully

accurate or descriptive but also they have a complicated history in terms of gender studies (which have traditionally relegated women's practices to the realm of the "private"). For more on the field and these categories, see Ando and Rüpke 2015.

9 Some scholars, like Pritchard, have argued that "privatizing" religion is a misnomer for the Reformation period, despite numerous discourses to that effect from reformers advocating for doctrines of personal salvation. Religion and religious debate were still recognized as public practices and the reformers still called for public argumentation. In this case, I mean "privatization" in the sense that it relates to the cliché, with religion becoming increasingly associated with independent/individual judgment.

10 For more on the influence of the Protestant Reformation on the founding of the United States, see Miller 2012.

11 For further discussion, see Nimmo and Fergusson 2016, 201. The Uniformity Act also authorized the English-language Common Book of Prayer, whereas previously the content of service books had been controlled by local officials.

12 That is, provided no one religious group infringed upon the rights of others.

13 In some of his unpublished letters, Locke is decisive that "the great business of Religion is to glorify God and find favor with him" and "[t]he end of a religious society (as has already been said) is the public worship of God, and, by means thereof, the acquisition of eternal life. All discipline ought therefore to tend to that end, and all ecclesiastical laws to be thereunto confined" (Perry 2011, 113–4). I use "religious institutions" here in recognition of Locke's larger arguments advocating for the building of synagogues. For more on this, see his *Letter Concerning Toleration.*

14 For an excellent discussion of Jefferson's views on Christianity, see Smith 1990; for Jefferson's engagement with Islam, see Spellberg 2013.

15 Kevin Schilbrack's *Philosophy and the Study of Religions: A Manifesto* (2014) is an excellent resource for any students interested in reading more about this issue.

16 Elsewhere, James compared the human capacity for belief to a shrieking dog on a vivisectionist's table, an animal unsure of why it suffers but aware that it must be for a reason greater than any it can comprehend. James' analogy to vivisection is found in an 1875 *Nation* article: "If his [the dog's] dark mind could be enlightened, and if he were a heroic dog, he would religiously acquiesce in his own sacrifice" (James 1875, 366–7). For discussion of this passage and its bearing on James' definition of religion, see Myers 2001, 449.

17 According to Google Ngram, references to "belief" across scholarship and literary genres reached its peak in the late nineteenth century: https://books.google.com/ngrams/graph?content=belief&year_start=1700&year_end=2017&corpus=15&smoothing=3&share=&direct_url=t1%3B%2Cbelief%3B%2Cc0 (accessed July 16, 2016).

18 Thank you to Jaswinder Bolina and Justin Ritzinger for their helpful comments on this piece.

Chapter 8

1 No exact number exists for the death toll, but the French Wars of Religion, which lasted from 1562 to 1598, alone killed between two and four million.

2 Numerous scholars have argued for this position. For one example, see Talal Asad, "The Construction of Religion as an Anthropological Category," in *Genealogies of Religion: Discipline and Reasons of Power in Christianity and Islam* (1993, 42–43).

3 In fact, the first use of the word "secular" can be traced to the Treaty of Westphalia (1648), which brought an end to the Wars of Religion. The treaty uses the word "secularity" to describe "the conversion of an ecclesiastical or religious institution or its property to sovereigns, princes or lay people" (See Taylor 2005, 131).

4 The phrase, "migration of the holy," comes from the work of John Bossy. Like Bossy and William Cavanaugh, what I am suggesting here is that it was only after the Reformation that the word "religion" began to take on its modern connotations as something distinct from the "secular" state and that this development expands, rather than eclipses, the theological ambitions of Western Christendom and its ecumenical aims. I am not suggesting that the Wars of Religion gave birth to the secular West, but that they were used by scholars and philosophers as a justification to expand the theological ambitions of Christians beyond the traditional constraints of confessional doctrine.

5 In this brief summary of Smart's position, I am leaving out many other details and texts that contributed this development. For a more detailed account, including discussion on Smart's seminal text, *Working Paper 36*, see Barnes 2000, 317–24.

6 Smart categorized the first three as parahistorical and the last four as historical.

7 As Tomoko Masuzawa notes, Smart's work is part of a larger turn toward phenomenology that began at the turn of the twentieth century and included other thinkers such as Ernst Troeltsch. See Masuzawa 2005.

8 With this emphasis on Smart, I am not trying to privilege the intellectual origins of religious studies its social historical influences. I am focusing on Smart because he was the key to push the idea of a new religious education. Although space does not permit a discussion of the issue here, many great studies have shown how US and British foreign policy in the twentieth century contributed immensely to the rise of religious studies. For instance, see Dolezalova, Luther, and Papousek 2001.

Chapter 10

1 I'm sure you can think of all sorts of objections to this assumption. I'll leave you to it so as to get back to our larger discussion of skepticism, atheism, and religion.

2 According to Smith, the initial meaning of belief lies in the medieval Anglo-Saxon term *leof* or *liof* (dear). Compare, for example, the similarities between "belief" and "beloved" (Smith 1979, 106; Lopez 1998, 22). Likewise the Latin word *credo* stems from the root *cor*, or *cordis*, (heart) and translates as "I set my heart on" or "I give my heart to" (Smith 1979, 76). Within the context of Christianity in particular, these older definitions are particularly relevant to the creedal statements that historically serve as the nucleus of religious beliefs and guide the possible approaches taken to evaluate religious doctrines, narratives, and practices. A direct and somewhat recent shift has occurred whereby "belief in x" is no longer conceptualized as a statement of affiliation but instead as absolute truth. Think about the difference that might be apparent if the statement, "I believe in God" means "I love God," or "I am beloved by God" as opposed to "God exists."

3 This lecture draws from Spong's 2009 bestselling book, *Eternal Life: A New Vision – Beyond Religion, Beyond Theism, Beyond Heaven and Hell.* The lecture can be viewed online at https://www.youtube.com/watch?v=qhAmYJgbFqk.

4 Watch the clip of this speech from August 6, 2015, at http://www.cc.com/video-clips/ss6u07/the-daily-show-with-jon-stewart-uncensored---three-different-kinds-of-bulls--t. In Stewart's assessment, the Bullshitocracy takes three forms: (1) making bad things sound like good things (such as naming the overt monitoring of Americans' personal data the Patriot Act); (2) hiding bad things under mountains of bullshit (as in the lengthy user agreements issued by companies like iTunes); and (3) infinite possibility (for example, the excuse that a consensus must be reached on climate change before action is taken).

5 False dilemma: the personal is always political.

6 Jim Bob and Michelle Duggar have nineteen children (ten boys and nine girls) all of whose names begin with the letter *J*.

Bibliography

Introduction

Dawkins, Richard (2008). *The God Delusion*. New York: Houghton Mifflin.
Locke, John (2003). *Two Treatises of Government and a Letter Concerning Toleration*. Edited by Ian Shapiro. New Haven, CT: Yale University Press.

Chapter 1

Asad, Talal (1993). *Genealogies of Religion: Discipline and Reasons of Power in Christianity and Islam*. Baltimore, MD: Johns Hopkins University Press.
Banerjee, Neela (2007). "Outed Pastor 'Completely Heterosexual.'" *New York Times*, February 7. Available at http://www.nytimes.com/2007/02/07/us/07haggard.html?rref=collection%2Ftimestopic%2FHaggard%2C%20Ted&action=click&contentCollection=timestopics&region=stream&module=stream_unit&version=latest&contentPlacement=42&pgtype=collection.
Bellah, Robert, Richard Madsen, William Sullivan, Ann Swidler, and Steven Tipton (1985). *Habits of the Heart: Individualism and Commitment in American Life*. New York: Harper and Row.
Chaves, Mark (2011). *American Religion: Contemporary Trends*. Princeton, NJ: Princeton University Press.
Cimino, Richard, and Don Lattin (1998). *Shopping for Faith: American Religion in the New Millennium*. San Francisco, CA: Jossey-Bass.
Clark, Lynn Schofield (2003). *From Angels to Aliens: Teenagers, the Media, and the Supernatural*. New York: Oxford University Press.
Davie, Jody Shapiro (1995). *Women in the Presence: Constructing Community and Seeking Spirituality in Mainline Protestantism*. Philadelphia: University of Pennsylvania Press.
Durkheim, Emile (1965). *The Elementary Forms of the Religious Life*. Translated by Joseph Ward Swain. New York: Free Press.
Fuller, Robert (2001). *Spiritual, but Not Religious: Understanding Unchurched America*. New York: Oxford University Press.
Hammond, Phillip (1992). *Religion and Personal Autonomy: The Third Disestablishment in America*. Columbia: South Carolina University Press.
Jagel, Katie (2013). "Poll Results: Exorcism." *YouGov: What the World Thinks*, September 17. Available at http://today.yougov.com/news/2013/09/17/poll-results-exorcism/.
Johnson, Jessica (2015). "Coming Under Conviction Online to Bodily Affect and Political Effect." Paper Presentation. American Academy of Religion Annual Conference, Atlanta, GA, November.

Johnson, Jessica (2018). *Biblical Porn: Sex, Affect, and Evangelical Empire.* Durham, NC: Duke University Press.

Kosmin, Barry, Ariela Keysar, Ryan Cragun, and Juham Navarro-Rivera (2009). *American Nones: The Profile of the No Religion Population.* Hartford, CT: Trinity College.

Lopez, Donald, Jr. (1998). "Belief." In *Critical Terms for Religious Studies.* Edited by Mark C. Taylor. Chicago, IL: University of Chicago Press, pp. 21–35.

Martin, Craig (2014). *Capitalizing Religion: Ideology and the Opiate of the Bourgeoisie.* London: Bloomsbury Press.

McCloud, Sean (2007). "Liminal Subjectivities and Religious Change: Circumscribing Giddens for the Study of American Religion." *Journal of Contemporary Religion* 22 (3): 295–309.

McGuire, Meredith B. (2008). *Lived Religion: Faith and Practice in Everyday Life.* New York: Oxford University Press.

Orsi, Robert (1993). "Forum: The Decade Ahead in Scholarship." *Religion and American Culture: A Journal of Interpretation* 3 (1): 1–8.

Orsi, Robert A (1997). "Everyday Miracles: The Study of Lived Religion." In *Lived Religion in America: Toward a History of Practice.* Edited by David D. Hall. Princeton, NJ: Princeton University Press, pp. 3–21.

Pew Research Center (2009). "Many Americans Mix Multiple Faiths." http://www.pewforum.org/2009/12/09/many-americans-mix-multiple-faiths/

Roof, Wade Clark (1993). *A Generation of Seekers: The Spiritual Journeys of the Baby Boom Generation.* San Francisco, CA: HarperSanFrancisco.

Roof, Wade Clark (1999). *Spiritual Marketplace: Baby Boomers and the Remaking of American Religion.* Princeton, NJ: Princeton University Press.

Roof, Wade Clark, and William McKinney (1987). *American Mainline Religion: Its Changing Shape and Future.* Brunswick, NJ: Rutgers.

Siegel, Taggart (1986). *Blue Collar and Buddha.* Portland, OR: Siegel Productions.

Swidler, Ann (2001). *Talk of Love: How Culture Matters.* Chicago, IL: University of Chicago Press.

Taylor, Humphrey (2003). *The Religious and Other Beliefs of Americans 2003.* Rochester, NY: Harris Interactive.

Wuthnow, Robert (1988). *The Restructuring of American Religion.* Princeton, NJ: Princeton University Press.

Chapter 2

Alsultany, Evelyn (2012). *Arabs and Muslims in the Media: Race and Representation After 9/11.* New York: New York University Press.

Armstrong, Karen (2002). *Islam: A Short History.* New York: Random House.

Asad, Talal (1993). *Genealogies of Religion: Discipline and Reasons of Power in Christianity and Islam.* Baltimore, MD: Johns Hopkins University Press.

Asad, Talal (2003). *Formations of the Secular: Christianity, Islam, Modernity.* Stanford: Stanford University Press.

Asad, Talal (2007). *On Suicide Bombing.* New York: Columbia University Press.

Asad, Talal, Wendy Brown, Judith Butler, and Saba Mahmood (2013). *Is Critique Secular? Blasphemy, Injury, and Free Speech*. New York: Fordham University Press.

Brown, Wendy (2006). *Regulating Aversion: Tolerance in the Age of Identity and Empire*. Princeton: Princeton University Press.

Buruma, Ian, and Margalit Avishai (2004). *Occidentalism: The West in the Eyes of Its Enemies*. New York: Penguin Press.

Cavanaugh, William T. (2009). *The Myth of Religious Violence: Secular Ideology and the Roots of Modern Conflict*. Oxford: Oxford University Press.

Collins, Randall (2008). *Violence: A Micro-Sociological Theory*. Princeton, NJ: Princeton University Press.

Dawkins, Richard (2006). *The God Delusion*. New York: Houghton Mifflin.

Dennett, Daniel (2006). *Breaking the Spell: Religion as a Natural Phenomenon*. New York: Viking.

Fernando, Mayanthi L. (2014). *The Republic Unsettled: Muslim French and the Contradictions of Secularism*. Durham, NC: Duke University Press.

Fitzgerald, Timothy (2003). *The Ideology of Religious Studies*. Oxford: Oxford University Press.

Fitzgerald, Timothy (2007). *Discourse on Civility and Barbarity: A Critical History of Religion and Related Categories*. New York: Oxford University Press.

Gottschalk, Peter, and Gabriel Greenberg (2008). *Islamophobia: Making Muslims the Enemy*. Lanham, MD: Rowman & Littlefield.

Harris, Sam (2004). *The End of Faith: Religion, Terror and the Future of Reason*. New York: W. W. Norton.

Harris, Sam (2006). *Letter to a Christian Nation*. New York: Random House.

Harris, Sam (2011). *The Moral Landscape: How Science Can Determine Human Values*. New York: Simon & Schuster.

Harris, Sam (2014). *Waking Up: A Guide to Spirituality without Religion*. New York: Simon & Schuster.

Harris, Sam, and Maajid Nawaz (2014). *Islam and the Future of Tolerance: A Dialogue*. Cambridge, MA: Harvard University Press.

Hirsi Ali, Ayaan (2008a). *The Caged Virgin: An Emancipation Proclamation for Women and Islam*. New York: Atria Books.

Hirsi Ali, Ayaan (2015a). "A Fiery Dissenter Rethinks Her Views." *The New York Times* March 25. Available at http://nytlive.nytimes.com/womenintheworld/2015/03/25/a-fiery-dissenter-rethinks-her-views/

Hirsi Ali, Ayaan (2008b). *Infidel*. New York: Atria Books.

Hirsi Ali, Ayaan (2011). *Nomad*. Toronto: Vintage Canada.

Hirsi Ali, Ayaan (2015b). *Heretic: Why Islam Needs a Reformation Now*. Toronto: Alfred A. Knopf Canada. Kindle Edition.

Hitchens, Christopher (2007). *God Is Not Great: How Religion Poisons Everything*. Toronto: McClelland & Stewart.

Hughes, Aaron W. (2013). *Muslim Identities: An Introduction to Islam*. New York: Columbia University Press.

Huntington, Samuel (1996). *The Clash of Civilizations and the Remaking of the World Order*. New York: Simon & Schuster Paperbacks.

Juegensmeyer, Mark, Margo Kitts, and Michael Jerryson, eds. (2013). *Handbook of Religion and Violence*. New York: Oxford University Press.

King, Richard (1999). *Orientalism and Religion: Postcolonial Theory, India and "the Mystic East."* London: Routledge.

Kumar, Deepa (2012). *Islamophobia and the Politics of Empire*. Chicago, IL: Haymarket Books.

Kundnani, Arun (2015). *The Muslims Are Coming: Islamophobia, Extremism, and the Domestic War on Terror*. London: Verso.

Lau, Kimberly (2000). *New Age Capitalism: Making Money East of Eden*. Philadelphia: University of Pennsylvania Press.

Lewis, Bernard (1990). "The Roots of Muslim Rage." *Atlantic Monthly* (September): 47–60.

Lincoln, Bruce (2003). *Holy Terrors: Thinking About Religion after September 11*. Chicago, IL: University of Chicago Press.

Lockman, Zachary (2009). *Contending Visions of the Middle East: The History and Politics of Orientalism*. 2nd ed. Cambridge, UK: Cambridge University Press, 2009.

Maher, Bill (2014a). "Ben Affleck, Sam Harris and Bill Maher Debate Radical Islam." YouTube October 6. Available at https://www.youtube.com/watch?v=vln9D81eO60.

Maher, Bill (2014b). "Real Time with Bill Maher." YouTube September 26. Available at https://www.youtube.com/watch?v=JDFrNQAjDYA.

Mahmood, Saba (2005). *Politics of Piety: The Islamic Revival and the Feminist Subject*. Princeton, NJ: Princeton University Press.

Mahmood, Saba (2015). *Religious Difference in a Secular Age: A Minority Report*. Princeton, NJ: Princeton University Press.

Mamdani, Mahmood (2004). *Good Muslim, Bad Muslim: American, the Cold War, and the Roots of Terror*. New York: Pantheon Books.

March, Andrew (2009). *Islam and Liberal Citizenship: The Search for an Overlapping Consensus*. New York: Oxford University Press.

Martin, Craig (2010). *Masking Hegemony: A Genealogy of Liberalism, Religion and the Private Sphere*. London, UK: Equinox.

Martin, Craig (2012). *A Critical Introduction to the Study of Religion*. Sheffield, UK: Equinox.

Martin, Craig (2014). *Capitalizing Religion: Ideology and the Opiate of the Bourgeois*. London: Bloomsbury.

Martin, Craig, and Russell T. McCutcheon, eds. (2012). *Religious Experience: A Reader*. Sheffield, UK: Equinox.

Massad, Joseph A. (2015). *Islam in Liberalism*. Chicago, IL: University of Chicago Press.

Masuzawa, Tomoko (2005). *The Invention of World Religions: Or, How European Universalism Was Preserved in the Language of Pluralism*. Chicago, IL: University of Chicago Press.

McCutcheon, Russell T. (2001). *Critics Not Caretakers: Redescribing the Public Study of Religion*. Albany, NY: SUNY Press.

McCutcheon, Russell T. (2007). *Studying Religion: An Introduction*. London, UK: Equinox Publishing.

Nongbri, Brent (2013). *Before Religion: A History of a Modern Concept*. New Haven, CT: Yale University Press.

Owen, Suzanne (2011). *The Appropriation of Native American Spirituality*. New York: Continuum.

Quillen, Ethan G. (2015). "Discourse Analysis and the Definition of Atheism." *Science, Religion and Culture* 2 (3): 25–35.

Ramadan, Tariq (2009). *In the Footsteps of the Prophet: Lessons from the Life of Muhammad*. New York: Oxford University Press.

Rushdie, Salman (2007). "'Imagine There's No Heaven'": A Letter to the Six
    Billionth World Citizen." In *The Portable Atheist: Essential Readings for the
    Nonbeliever*. Edited by C. Hitchens. Philadelphia, PA: De Capo, pp. 380–3.
Said, Edward (1979). *Orientalism*. New York: Vintage Books.
Saunders, Doug (2012). *The Myth of the Muslim Tide: Do Immigrants Threaten
    the West?* Toronto: Knopf Canada.
Selby, Jennifer (2014). "Un/veiling Women's Bodies: Secularism and Sexuality
    in Full-Face Veil Prohibitions in France and Québec." *Studies in Religion/
    Sciences Religieuses* 43 (3): 439–66.
Shaheen, Jack G. (2014). *Reel Bad Arabs: How Hollywood Vilifies a People,
    Revised Edition*. Northampton, MA: Olive Branch Press.
Shakman-Hurd, Elizabeth (2008). *The Politics of Secularism in International
    Relations*. Princeton, NJ: Princeton University Press.
Singleton, Mark (2010). *Yoga Body: The Origins of Modern Posture Practice*.
    New York: Oxford University Press.
Smith, Jonathan Z. (1982). "The Devil in Mr. Jones." In *Imagining
    Religion: From Babylon to Jonestown*. Chicago, IL: University of Chicago
    Press, 102–20.
Smith, Jonathan Z. (2004). "Religion, Religions, Religious." In *Relating
    Religion: Essays in the Study of Religion*. Chicago, IL: University of
    ChicagoPress.
Sullivan, Winnifred Fallers (2007). *The Impossibility of Religious Freedom*.
    Princeton, NJ : Princeton University Press.
Wallach-Scott, Joan (2010). *The Politics of the Veil*. Princeton, NJ: Princeton
    University Press.

Chapter 3

Arnal, William, and Russell McCutcheon (2013). *The Sacred Is
    the Profane: The Political Nature of "Religion."* Oxford: Oxford
    University Press.
Asad, Talal (2003). *Formations of the Secular: Christianity, Islam, Modernity*.
    Stanford: Stanford University Press.
Barrick, Audrey (2012). "Max Lucado Tells Christians Not to 'Freak Out' Ahead
    of Election; God Is in Control." *Christian Post*, August 13. Available at http://
    www.christianpost.com/news/max-lucado-tells-christians-not-to-freak-out-
    ahead-of-election-god-is-in-control-79950/.
Brosnan, S. F., H. Schiff, and F. B. M. de Waal (2005). "Tolerance for Inequity
    Increases with Social Closeness in Chimpanzees." *Proceedings of the
    Royal Society* B272 (1560): 253–8.
Delaney, Carol (2012). *Columbus and the Quest for Jerusalem: How Religion
    Drove the Voyages That Led to America*. New York: Free Press.
Editor (2010). "Trijicon, Inc. Offers to Voluntarily Remove Scripture References
    on All Products Destined for U.S. Military." *Defense & Aerospace
    Business*. February 3: 130.
Editorial Staff (2010). "Why People Embrace God before Elections."
    Investment Weekly News. November 13: 1600.
Foucault, Michel (1995). *Discipline and Punish: The Birth of the Prison*.
    Translated by Alan Sheridan. New York: Vintage Books.

Fraser, Benjamin James (2010). "Adaptation, Exaptation, By-Products, and Spandrels in Evolutionary Explanations of Morality." *Biological Theory* 5 (3): 223–7.

Gallese, V. (2001). "The 'Shared Manifold' Hypothesis: From Mirror Neurons to Empathy." In *Between Ourselves: Second-Person Issues in the Study of Consciousness*. Edited by E. Thompson. Thorverton: ImprintAcademic.

Herper, Matthew (2016). "Solving Pharma's Shkreli Problem." *Forbes*, 197 (2): 80–85.

Iacoboni, Marco (2009). "Imitation, Empathy, and Mirror Neurons." *Annual Review of Psychology* 60: 653–72.

Jancelewicz, Chris (2015). "Phil Robertson, 'Duck Dynasty' Star, Delivers Speech About Atheist Family Getting Raped and Killed." *Huffington Post*, March 24. Available at http://www.huffingtonpost.ca/2015/03/24/phil-robertson-duck-dynasty-hate-speech_n_6934164.html?.

Joyce, Richard (2000). "Darwinian Ethics and Error." *Biology and Philosophy* 15 (5): 713–32.

Joyce, Richard (2006). *The Evolution of Morality*. Cambridge: MIT Press.

Kaleem, Jaweed (2014). "Half of Americans Say God Plays a Role in Super Bowl Winner: Survey." *Huffington Post*, January 25. Available at http://www.huffingtonpost.com/2014/01/16/super-bowl-prayer_n_4605665.html.

Katz, L. D. (2000). *Evolutionary Origins of Morality: Cross-Disciplinary Perspectives*. Exeter: Imprint Academic.

Nongbri, Brent (2013). *Before Religion: A History of a Modern Concept*. New Haven, CT: Yale University Press.

Norenzayan, Ara (2013). *Big Gods: How Religion Transformed Cooperation and Conflict*. Princeton, NJ: Princeton University Press.

O'Connell, Kevin (2015). "CEO of Doom." *Dollars & Sense* 321: 4.

Pinto, Laura and Selena Nemorin (2014). "Who's the Boss? 'The Elf on the Shelf' and the Normalization of Surveillance." *Canadian Centre for Policy Alternatives*, December 1 Available at https://www.policyalternatives.ca/publications/commentary/who%E2%80%99s-boss.

Sharpton, Al, and Christopher Hitchens (2007). Public debate, New York Public Library. Available at http://library.fora.tv/2007/05/07/Al_Sharpton_and_Christopher_Hitchens.

Sontag, Susan (2003). *Regarding the Pain of Others*. New York: Picador.

Stephen, Andrew (2002). "Andrew Stephen Finds Americans Too Smug." *New Statesman*, July 15. Available at http://www.newstatesman.com/node/155916.

Stowers, Stanley (2011). "The Religion of Plant and Animal Offerings versus the Religion of Meanings, Essences, and Textual Mysteries." In *Ancient Mediterranean Sacrifice*. Edited by Jennifer Wright Knust and Zsuzsanna Varhelyi. Oxford: Oxford University Press, pp. 35–56.

de Waal, Frans (2006). *Primates and Philosophers: How Morality Evolved*. Princeton, NJ: Princeton University Press.

de Waal, Frans (2013). *The Bonobo and the Atheist: In Search of Humanism among the Primates*. New York: W. W. Norton.

Warneken, F. and M. Tomasello (2006). "Altruistic Helping in Human Infants and Young Chimpanzees." *Science* 311: 1301–3.

Weeks, William Earl (1996). *Building the Continental Empire: American Expansion from the Revolution to the Civil War*. Chicago, IL: Ivan R. Dee.

Whitehouse, Harvey (2004). *Modes of Religiosity: A Cognitive Theory of Religious Transmission*. Walnut Creek, CA: AltaMira Press.

Chapter 4

Alcoholics Anonymous (2004). *Twelve Steps and Twelve Traditions*. New York: Alcoholics Anonymous World Services, Inc.

Eck, Diana (2002). *A New Religious America: How a "Christian Country" Has Become the World's Most Religiously Diverse Nation*. San Francisco, CA: HarperSanFrancisco.

Eliade, Mircea (1957). *The Sacred and the Profane: The Nature of Religion*. San Diego, CA: Harcourt Brace Jovanovich.

Eliade, Mircea (1996). *Patterns in Comparative Religion*. New York: Sheed and Ward.

Esposito, John (2004). *Islam: The Straight Path*. 3rd ed. Oxford: Oxford University Press.

Fisher, Mary Pat (2013). *Living Religions*. 9th ed. New York: Pearson.

Krulwich, Robert and Jad Abumrad (2013). "Sleep." *RadioLab*, March 15. Available at http://www.radiolab.org/story/91528-sleep/.

Lincoln, Bruce (2003). *Holy Terrors: Thinking About Religion after September 11*. Chicago, IL: University of Chicago Press.

Lofton, Kathryn (2011). *Oprah: Gospel of an Icon*. Berkeley: University of California Press.

Obama, Barack (2015). "Remarks by President at National Prayer Breakfast." The White House. February 5. Available at https://www.whitehouse.gov/the-press-office/2015/02/05/remarks-president-national-prayer-breakfast.

Otto, Rudolph (1923). *The Idea of the Holy*. Oxford: Oxford University Press.

Parkinson, John (2011). "Congress Pays Tribute to 9/11, Sings 'God Bless America' Again," ABC News, September 12. Available at http://abcnews.go.com/blogs/politics/2011/09/congress-pays-tribute-to-911-sings-god-bless-america-again/.

Chapter 5

Ando, Clifford and Jörg Rüpke (2015). *Public and Private in Ancient Mediterranean Law and Religion*. Berlin: Wouter de Gruyter.

Arnal, William E. and Russell T. McCutcheon (2013). *The Sacred Is the Profane: The Political Nature of "Religion."* Oxford: Oxford University Press.

Asad, Talal (1993). *Genealogies of Religion: Discipline and Reasons of Power in Christianity and Islam*. Baltimore, MD: Johns Hopkins University Press.

Asad, Talal (2003). *Formations of the Secular: Christianity, Islam, Modernity*. Stanford: Stanford University Press.

Bourdieu, Pierre (1990). *The Logic of Practice*. Stanford: Stanford University Press.

Bourdieu, Pierre (1991). *Language and Symbolic Power*. Translated by Gino Raymond and Matthew Adamson. Cambridge, MA: Harvard University Press.

Bourdieu, Pierre (1993). *The Field of Cultural Production: Essays on Art and Literature*. Edited by Randal Johnson. New York: Columbia University Press.

Bourdieu, Pierre (2000). *Outline of a Theory of Practice*. Translated by Richard Nice. Cambridge: Cambridge University Press.

Brubaker, Rogers (2004). *Ethnicity without Groups*. Cambridge, MA: Harvard University Press.

Cappon, Lester J., ed. (1988). *The Adams-Jefferson Letters: The Complete Correspondence*. Chapel Hill, NC: University of North Carolina Press.

Cavanaugh, Willian T. (2009). *The Myth of Religious Violence: Secular Ideology and the Roots of Modern Conflict*. Oxford: Oxford University Press.

Geertz, Clifford (1973). *The Interpretation of Cultures*. New York: Basic Books.

Guelzo, Allen C. (2003). *Abraham Lincoln: Redeemer*. Grand Rapids, MI: William D. Eerdmans.

Holmes, Jack (2016). "Bill O'Reilly Finally Proved That Obama Has 'Secret Muslim Ties.'" *Esquire*, July 7. Available at http://www.esquire.com/news-politics/videos/a46511/bill-oreilly-obama-muslim/.

James, William (1985). *The Varieties of Religious Experience*. Cambridge, MA: Harvard University Press.

Kaiser, David Aram (1999). *Romanticism, Aesthetics, and Nationalism*. Cambridge: Cambridge University Press.

Lincoln, Bruce (2009). *Holy Terrors: Thinking About Religion after September 11*. Chicago, IL: University of Chicago Press.

Locke, John (1997). *Political Essays*. Edited by Mark Goldie. Cambridge: Cambridge University Press.

Lopez, Donald S. (1998). "Belief." In *Critical Terms for Religious Studies*. Edited by Mark C. Taylor. Chicago, IL: University of Chicago Press, pp. 21–35.

Mack, Burton (2008). *Myth and the Christian Nation: A Social Theory of Religion*. London: Equinox.

Mansfield, Stephen (2012). *Lincoln's Battle with God: A President's Struggle with Faith and What It Meant for America*. Nashville, TN: Thomas Nelson.

McCutcheon, Russel T. (2001). *Critics Not Caretakers: Redescribing the Public Study of Religion*. Albany: State University of New York Press.

Miller, Nicolas P. (2012). *The Religious Roots of the First Amendment: Dissenting Protestants and the Separation of Church and State*. Oxford: Oxford University Press.

Milton, George Fort (1930). *The Age of Hate: Andrew Johnson and the Radicals*. New York, NY: Coward-McCann.

Myers, Gerald Eugene (2001). *William James: His Life and Thought*. New Haven, CT: Yale University Press.

Nietzsche, Friedrich (1996). *Human, All Too Human: A Book for Free Spirits*. Translated by R. J. Hollingdale. Cambridge: Cambridge University Press.

Nimmo, Paul T. and David A.S. Fergusson (2016). *The Cambridge Companion to Reformed Theology*. Cambridge: Cambridge University Press.

"Obama Strongly Denounces Former Pastor" (2016). Associated Press, April 29. Available at http://www.nbcnews.com/id/24371827/.

Perry, John (2011). *The Pretenses of Loyalty: Locke, Liberal Theory, and American Political Theology*. Oxford: Oxford University Press.

Pritchard, Elizabeth (2013). *Religion in Public*. Stanford: Stanford University Press.

Schatzki, Theodore R. (2002). *The Site of the Social: A Philosophical Account of the Constitution of Social Life and Change.* University Park: Pennsylvania State University Press.

Schilbrack, Kevin (2014). *Philosophy and the Study of Religions: A Manifesto.* Chichester, West Sussex: Wiley-Blackwell.

Schleiermacher, Friedrich (1996). *On Religion: Speeches to Its Cultured Despisers.* Cambridge: Cambridge University Press.

Sheeler, Jason (2014). "Rihanna Takes a Moment." *Glamour* (UK) (January): 175–81.

Smith, Jonathan Z. (1978). *Map Is Not Territory: Studies in the History of Religions.* Chicago, IL: Chicago University Press.

Smith, Jonathan Z. (1982). *Imagining Religion: From Babylon to Jonestown.* Chicago, IL: University of Chicago Press.

Smith, Jonathan Z. (1990). *Drudgery Divine: On the Comparison of Early Christianities and the Religions of Late Antiquity.* Chicago, IL: University of Chicago Press.

Smith, Jonathan Z. (1992). *To Take Place: Toward Theory in Ritual.* Chicago, IL: University of Chicago Press.

Smith, Jonathan Z. (2004) *Relating Religion: Essays in the Study of Religion.* Chicago, IL: University of Chicago Press.

Sorkin, David (2011). *The Religious Enlightenment: Protestants, Jews, and Catholics from London to Vienna.* Princeton, NJ: Princeton University Press.

Spellberg, Denise A. (2013). *Thomas Jefferson's Qur'an: Islam and the Founders.* New York: Knopf Doubleday.

Stowers, Stanley Kent (1997). *A Rereading of Romans: Justice, Jews, and Gentiles.* New Haven, CT: Yale University Press.

Stowers, Stanley Kent (2007). "The Concepts of 'Religion,' 'Political Religion' and the Study of Nazism." *Journal of Contemporary History* 42: 9–24.

Stowers, Stanley Kent (2008). "The Ontology of Religion." In *Introducing Religion.* Edited by Willi Braun and Russell T. McCutcheon. London: Equinox, pp. 434–449.

Thomasos, Christine (2013). "Rihanna Talks Relationship with God." *The Christian Post*, December 5. Available at http://www.christianpost.com/news/rihanna-talks-relationship-with-god-110109.

Thurow, Glen E. (1976). *Abraham Lincoln and American Political Religion.* Albany: State University of New York Press.

Weber, Max (2013). *From Max Weber: Essays in Sociology.* London: Routledge.

Chapter 6

Bayly, S. (1989). *Saints, Goddesses, and Kings: Muslims and Christians in South Indian Society, 1700–1900.* Cambridge: Cambridge University Press.

Bellah, R. N., et al. (1985). *Habits of the Heart: Individualism and Commitment in American Life.* Berkeley: University of California Press.

Bruinius, H. (2015). "Why These Americans Are 'Done' with Church but Not with God." *Christian Science Monitor* 1 (December 1).

Available at. http://www.csmonitor.com/USA/Society/2015/1219/
Why-these-Americans-are-done-with-church-but-not-with-God.

"Dual Religious Identity: Can One Practice Two Religions?" (2016). *Dharma World* 43 (Jan.–Mar.). Available at http://www.rk-world.org/dharmaworld/
dw_2016janmar.aspx.

Eaton, R. M. (1993). *The Rise of Islam and the Bengal Frontier, 1204–1760.* Berkeley: University of California Press.

Gajwani, S. L. (2000). *A Sufi Galaxy: Sufi Qalandar Hazrat Sai Qutab Ali Shah, His Spiritual Successors and Select Disciples – Sufi Saint of the Present Times.* Ulhas Nagar, Maharashtra: H. M. Damodar.

Hall, D. D. (1989). *Worlds of Wonder; Days of Judgment: Popular Religious Belief in Early New England.* Cambridge, MA: Harvard University Press.

Iknoor Singh v. John McHugh et al. 1:2014cv01906 (D. Colo. 2015). Available at https://www.aclu.org/sites/default/files/field_document/singh_decision.pdf.

Jain, P. (2016). "MP: Muslim Kids Participate in Surya Namaskar." *Hindustan Times,* January 13. Available at http://www.hindustantimes.
com/bhopal/mp-muslim-kids-participate-in-surya-namaskar/story-
f6gYXyq9m8ZRzUN4OwjRNP.html.

Johnson, I. (2014). "Chinese Atheists? What the Pew Survey Gets Wrong." *New York Review of Books,* March 24. Available at http://www.nybooks.
com/daily/2014/03/24/chinese-atheists-pew-gets-wrong/.

Masuzawa, T. (2005). *The Invention of World Religions, or, How European Universalism Was Preserved in the Language of Pluralism.* Chicago, IL: University of Chicago Press.

Nongbri, B. (2013). *Before Religion: A History of a Modern Concept.* New Haven, CT: Yale University Press.

Patel, R. (2015). "Why This Diwali Observing Hindu Family Also Celebrates Christmas." *Washington Post,* December 21. Available at https://www.
washingtonpost.com/news/parenting/wp/2015/12/21/why-this-diwali-
observing-hindu-family-also-celebrates-christmas/.

Pew Research Center (2012). "'Nones' on the Rise: One-in-Five Adults Have No Religious Affiliation." *Pew Forum,* October 9. Available at http://www.
pewforum.org/files/2012/10/NonesOnTheRise-full.pdf.

Smith, J. Z. (1998). "Religion, Religions, Religious." In *Critical Terms for Religious Studies.* Edited by M C. Taylor. Chicago, IL: University of Chicago Press, pp. 269–84.

Speckhardt, R. (2015). "Counting the Godless." *Huffington Post,* June 16. Available at http://www.huffingtonpost.com/roy-speckhardt/counting-the-
godless_b_7586600.html.

Chapter 8

Asad, T. (1993). *Genealogies of Religion: Discipline and Reasons of Power in Christianity and Islam.* Baltimore, MD: Johns Hopkins University Press.

Aspin, D. N. (1983). "Church Schools, Religious Education and the Multi-ethnic Community." *Journal of Philosophy of Education* 17: 229–40.

Barnes, P. L. (1987). "Light from the East? Ninian Smart and the Christian-Buddhist Encounter." *Scottish Journal of Theology* 40: 67–83.

Barnes, P. L. (1994). "Rudolf Otto and the Limits of Religious Description."
    Religious Studies 30: 219–30.
Barnes, P. L. (1997). "Religion, Religionism and Religious Education: Fostering
    Tolerance and Truth in Schools." *Journal of Education and Christian Belief*
    1: 7–23.
Barnes, P. L. (2000). "Ninian Smart and the Phenomenological Approach to
    Religious Education." *Religion* 30: 315–32.
Barnes, P. L. (2001). "The Contribution of Professor Ninian Smart to Religious
    Education." *Religion* 31: 317–19.
Bates, D. (1994). "Christianity, Culture and Other Religions (Part 1): The
    Origins of the Study of World Religions in English Education." *British
    Journal of Religious Education* 17: 5–18.
Bodin, J. (2008). *Colloquium of the Seven About Secrets of the Sublime.*
    Translated by Marion Leathers Kuntz. Pennsylvania: Penn State
    University Press.
Bossy, J. (1985). *Christianity in the West 1400–1700.* Oxford: Oxford
    University Press.
Cavanaugh, W. T. (2009). *The Myth of Religious Violence: Secular Ideology and
    the Roots of Modern Conflict.* New York: Oxford University Press.
Collins, E. (2015). "Kasich Calls for New Federal Agency to
    Promote Judeo-Christian Values." *Politico*, November
    17. Available at http://www.politico.com/story/2015/11/
    john-kasich-judeo-christian-agency-216001#ixzz4EglJ0nTy.
Cox, E. (1983). *Problems and Possibilities for Religious Education.*
    London: Hodder & Stoughton.
Dolezalova, I., H. M. Luther, and D. Papousek (2001). *The Academic Study
    of Religion during the Cold War: East and West.* Toronto: University of
    Toronto Press.
Eliade, M. (1958). *Patterns in Comparative Religion.* Translated by Rosemary
    Sheed. London: Sheed and Ward.
Fitzgerald, T. (2000). *The Ideology of Religious Studies.* Oxford: Oxford
    University Press.
Fitzgerald, T. (2007). *Discourse on Civility and Barbarity: A Critical History of
    Religion and Related Categories.* Oxford: Oxford University Press.
Fitzgerald, T. (2011). *Religion and Politics in International Relations: The
    Modern Myth.* New York: Continuum.
Jackson, R. (2004). *Rethinking Religious Education and Plurality: Issues in
    Diversity and Pedagogy.* New York: RoutledgeFalmer.
Lincoln, B. (1989). *Discourse and the Construction of Society: Comparative
    Studies of Myth, Ritual, and Classification.* Oxford: Oxford
    University Press.
Masuzawa. T. (2005). *The Invention of World Religions: Or, How European
    Universalism Was Preserved in the Language of Pluralism.* Chicago,
    IL: University of Chicago Press.
McCutcheon, R. T. (2007). *Studying Religion: An Introduction.* Bristol,
    CT: Equinox Publishing.
Moore, L. and A. Mudd . (2016). "Religious Literacy: Traditions
    and Scriptures." *Edx.* Available at https://www.edx.org/course/
    religious-literacy-traditions-scriptures-harvardx-hds-3221-1x
Obama, O. (2009). "Nobel Prize for Peace Lecture." *American Rhetoric.*
    Available at https://www.AmericanRhetoric.com.

Otto, R. (1958). *The Idea of the Holy.* Translated by J. W. Harvey. New York: Oxford University.

"Pluralism & Religious Diversity Week: March 23–28." *University of Calgary.* Available at https://www.ucalgary.ca/fsc/programs-services/pluralism-week/ 2015.

Preus, S. J. (1987). *Explaining Religion: Criticism and Theory from Bodin to Freud.* New Haven: Yale University Press.

Sharpe, E. F. (1975). *Comparative Religion: A History.* London: Duckworth.

Sharpe, E. F. (1983). *Understanding Religion.* London: Duckworth.

Smart, N. (1958). *Reasons and Faiths.* London: Routledge & Kegan Paul.

Smart, N. (1964). *Doctrine and Argument in Indian Philosophy.* London: Allen and Unwin.

Smart, N. (1966). *The Teacher and Christian Belief.* Cambridge: Clarke.

Smart, N. (1968). *Secular Education and the Logic of Religion.* London: Faber and Faber.

Smart, N. (1971). *The Religious Experience of Mankind.* London: Collins.

Smart, N. (1972). "Comparative Religion Clichés: Crushing the Clichés about Comparative Religion and Then Accentuating the Positive Value of the New Religious Education." *Learning for Living* 12 (2): 4–7.

Smart, N. (1973a). *The Phenomenon of Religion.* London: Macmillan.

Smart, N. (1973b). *The Science of Religion and the Sociology of Knowledge.* Princeton, NJ: Princeton University Press.

Smart, N. (1979). *The Phenomenon of Christianity.* London: Collins.

Smart, N. (1981). *Beyond Ideology: Religion and the Future of Western Civilization.* London: Collins.

Smart, N. (1987). *Religion and the Western Mind.* New York: State University of New York Press.

Smart, N. (1989). *The World's Religions.* Cambridge: Cambridge University Press.

Smart, N. (1993). "Clarity and Imagination as Buddhist Means to Virtue." In *Can Virtue be Taught.* Edited by Barbara Darling-Smith. Notre Dame: University of Notre Dame Press, pp. 125–36.

Smart, N. (1995). "The Values of Religious Studies." *Journal of Beliefs and Values* 16: 7–10.

Smart, N. (1996). *Dimensions of the Sacred: An Anatomy of the World's Beliefs.* Berkeley: University of California Press.

Smart, N. (1998a). "Methods in My Life." In *The Craft of Religious Studies.* Edited by Jon R. Stone. London: Macmillan, pp. 18–35.

Smart, N. (1998b). *Ninian Smart on World Religions, Volume 1: Religious Experience and Philosophical Analysis.* Edited by John J. Shepherd. Burlington: Ashgate.

Smart, N. (1999). *World Philosophies.* London: Routledge.

Spinoza, B. (2007). *Theological Political Treatise.* Translated by Jonathan Israel. Cambridge: Cambridge University Press.

Taylor, M. C. (2005). *After God.* Chicago: University of Chicago Press.

Templeton, E. (1999). "Religious Education in a Secular Pluralist Culture." *Religion, State & Society* 27:1: 73–81.

Van der Leeuw, G. (2014). *Religion in Essence and Manifestation: A Study in Phenomenology.* Princeton, NJ: Princeton University Press.

Wiebe, D. D. (2005). "Religious Studies." In *The Routledge Companion to the Study of Religion.* Edited by J. R. Hinnells. London: Routledge, pp. 98–124.

Chapter 9

Academy of Management (n.d.). "Academy of Management Division & Interest Group Domain Statements." Available at http://aom.org/Content.aspx?id=237#msr.

Fowler, James (1981). *Stages of Faith: The Psychology of Human Development and the Quest for Meaning*. New York: Harper & Row.

James, William (2002). *The Varieties of Religious Experience: A Study in Human Nature*. New York: Modern Library.

Lincoln, Bruce (1999). *Theorizing Myth: Narrative, Ideology, and Scholarship*. Chicago, IL: University of Chicago Press.

Smith, Wilfred Cantwell (1962). *The Meaning and End of Religion*. New York: Macmillan Press.

Tillich, Paul (1957). *The Dynamics of Faith*. New York: Harper & Row.

Chapter 10

Amarasingam, Amarnath, ed. (2010). *Religion and the New Atheists: A Critical Appraisal*. Leiden: Brill.

Asad, Talal (1993). *Genealogies of Religion: Discipline and Reasons of Power in Christianity and Islam*. Baltimore, MD: Johns Hopkins University Press.

Beattie, Tina (2008). *The New Atheists: The Twilight of Reason and the War on Religion*. New York: Orbis Books.

Clark, Lynn Schofield, and Jill Dierberg (2012). "New Trends, Looking Forward: Stephen Colbert and Late Night Comedy as a Source of Religion News." In *Handbook of Religion and the News*. Edited by Diane Winston. New York: Oxford University Press, pp. 97–112.

Cottee, Simon (2015). *The Apostates: When Muslims Leave Islam*. London: Hurst and Company.

Fitzgerald, Timothy (2000). *The Ideology of Religious Studies*. New York: Oxford University Press.

Frankfurt, Harry G. (2005). *On Bullshit*. Princeton, NJ: Princeton University Press.

Freud, Sigmund (1950). *Totem and Taboo*. New York: W. W. Norton.

Freud, Sigmund (1989). *The Future of an Illusion*. New York: W. W. Norton.

Hatch, Nathan O. (1989). *The Democratization of American Religion*. New Haven, CT: Yale University Press.

Hulsether, Mark (2008). "Why New Atheist Definitions of Religion Fail." In *The Edge of Reason: Science and Religion in Modern Society*. Edited by Alex Bentley. New York: Continuum Press, pp. 23–30.

Keane, Webb (2002). "Sincerity, 'Modernity,' and the Protestants." *Cultural Anthropology* 17 (1): 65–92.

Latour, Bruno (1993). *We Have Never Been Modern*. Cambridge: Harvard University Press.

Lindvall, Terry (2015). *God Mocks: A History of Religious Satire from the Hebrew Prophets to Stephen Colbert*. New York: New York University Press.

Lopez, Donald S., Jr. (1998). "Belief." In *Critical Terms for Religious Studies*. Edited by Mark C. Taylor. Chicago, IL: University of Chicago Press, pp. 21–35.

Martin, Craig (2014). *Capitalizing Religion: Ideology and the Opiate of the Bourgeois*. London: Bloomsbury Publishing.

Marx, Karl. (1970). *Critique of Hegel's 'Philosophy of Right'*. New York: Cambridge University Press.

Masuzawa, Tomoko (2005). *The Invention of World Religions: Or, How European Universalism Was Preserved in the Language of Pluralism*. Chicago, IL: University of Chicago Press.

McCutcheon, Russell T. (1997). *Manufacturing Religion: The Discourse on Sui Generis Religion and the Politics of Nostalgia*. New York: Oxford University Press.

McCutcheon, Russell T. (2003). *The Discipline of Religion: Structure, Meaning, Rhetoric*. New York: Routledge.

Modern, John Lardas (2011). *Secularism in Antebellum America*. Chicago, IL: University of Chicago Press.

Peters, Mark (2015). *Bull-shit [boo'l-shit]: A Lexicon*. New York: Three Rivers Press.

Smith, Christian, ed. (2003). *The Secular Revolution: Power, Interests, and Conflict in the Secularization of American Public Life*. Berkeley: University of California Press.

Smith, Jonathan Z. (2004). "What a Difference a Difference Makes." In *Relating Religion: Essays in the Study of Religion*. Chicago, IL: University of Chicago Press, pp. 251–302.

Smith, Wilfred Cantwell. (1977). *Belief and History*. Charlottesville: University of Virginia Press.

Smith, Wilfred Cantwell (1979). *Faith and Belief*. Princeton, NJ: Princeton University Press.

Taylor, Charles (1989). *Sources of the Self: The Making of the Modern Identity*. Cambridge: Harvard University Press.

Turner, James (1985). *Without God, without Creed: The Origins of Unbelief in America*. Baltimore, MD: Johns Hopkins University Press.

Warner, Michael (2002). *Publics and Counterpublics*. New York: Zone Books.

Young, Ralph (2015). *Dissent: The History of an American Idea*. New York: New York University Press.

Index